# THROUGH ADVERSITY

CW00517189

# THROUGH ADVERSITY

## The Fight for Rugby League in the RAF

### Damian Clayton
### with Daniel Abrahams

Scratching Shed Publishing Ltd

In memory of Bob Abrahams
*The pursuit of absolute justice*

# The Authors

Damian Clayton is a Warrant Officer in the Royal Air Force and has served his country both at home and overseas for the last 26 years. He captained the Royal Air Force at rugby league for a decade, gained numerous caps for Combined Services and ended his representative career as captain of the Great Britain Masters side against Australia in 2011.

Daniel Abrahams is the sports editor for *RAF News* and has worked as a journalist with the *Sunday Mirror* and other national newspapers for 20 years. This is his first book.

# Contents

# Dedication

To Lorraine: For your encouragement, guidance and enthusiasm throughout this epic journey. For your understanding and support even during your darkest hours. You have been, and continue to be, my inspiration.

To Connor: For looking after your mum and not once causing me a drama while I've been away. For providing us both with a level of pride and admiration I didn't think possible. The world really is your oyster; make the most of it and don't forget the silencer!

To Mum: For the many miles in the Mini and your never-ending support whatever the weather. For being both mum and dad, instilling our core values and making sure we didn't miss out on anything.

To Maurice and Thelma: For your humour, support and stability; the knowledge that you are there for us has been reassuring - thank you.

To my work colleagues: For the endless banter and ribbing - I only got there because of rugby league!

To my team-mates: Mateship - says it all. Enjoy that feeling and special bond you have as players. Believe me, it isn't the same after you hang up your boots.

To Dan: For your dedication and commitment to getting this story onto the shelves. The countless hours on the phone trying to interpret my dull Yorkshire tones and your real understanding of the class divide our great sport has experienced. You're a star my southern friend! Thank you.

# Foreword I

*By Kevin Sinfield*

THE game of rugby league needs people like Damian Clayton. People who are in many ways the lifeblood of the game, whose enthusiasm and infectious character drive the sport on at all levels.

I am lucky enough to have built up a great friendship with Damian over the past 18 months, but his involvement in the professional game goes back much further. I am certain, as a lot of people are, that the reason the RFL and the Armed Forces have such a great relationship is predominantly down to him.

It's not just symbolic that this book is coming out during such an important year for the game with the Armed Forces and professional World Cups in Britain, it is perfect. Perfect because the fight and immense character Damian has shown to get his game recognised and the tale that is told within these pages, is the sort of fight any side needs to lift such prestigious trophies.

I really got to know Damian during our first England

## Through Adversity

Elite Training Squad camp held at RAF Cranwell. He was so well prepared and enthusiastic, with such a keen interest I was immediately intrigued. Then to learn his story and find out what a tremendous character and gentlemen he is, well, it was a pleasure.

For us as players that first year at Cranwell was a big turning point. We outlined where we would like to go and our goals. The camp really brought the group together; it was a time for a lot of honesty and time to frame our plan to be ready and set for the back end of 2013.

There are so many comparisons between the game and the Armed Forces. We talk about a battle, but we are not putting our lives on the line. The fact that we have a superb link with the Armed Forces and we have a true appreciation of the work these amazing people do is great and it's been an absolute pleasure to give something back.

Before I knew Damian I always remember seeing him around. He would lead us out onto the pitch at Grand Final games or internationals. To see a friendly face and know that person cares about what you are doing when you are about to go out onto the field of play is always a good feeling.

As rugby league players, being in touch with the supporters is all part of our heritage. We are very respectful of what is happening and what is to come in the game and so many of us appreciate the journey and adversity Damian has faced for the game of rugby league.

He is one of the unsung heroes of sport. It's been a privilege for me to get to know him. I honestly believe rugby league, as a whole, should be really proud of him and his achievements.

*Kevin Sinfield, September 2013*

# Foreword II

## By Paul Sculthorpe

TO be asked to put down a few words as the foreword for this book was not only an honour because of the great rapport and now friendship I have had the pleasure of building with Damian Clayton, it was a chance to show my support for Service rugby league and to highlight the importance of its role within the modern game.

Within these pages is a story of one man's bravery, belligerence and belief in our game that has helped in part to drive it to the forefront of Military sport, culminating in a World Cup triumph in Australia in 2008.

There is also a great story of a life and successful career within the Military against a backdrop of determination and heartache by a man who is one of the good guys. His lovely wife Lorraine and son, Connor, are pretty special too.

I first met Damian at the Holiday Inn in Brighouse, Yorkshire, in 2005 - having been contacted by Wg Cdr Dean Andrew, himself a big rugby league man [be it Hull FC] - and was asked to take part in a flight in a Tornado jet.

The idea behind the flight and prospected media

coverage of the event was partly to promote Service rugby league, but also to build stronger ties between the pro game and the RAF. I was ideally placed, being the current Great Britain and St Helens captain.

Within an hour in Damian's company I felt like I had known him all my life. He is such an enthusiastic and easy going person with a real drive and love for the game - a pleasure to be around.

It was an honour to meet up with the RAF personnel at RAF Marham for the flight and to see the effort they put into our sport and, of course, to take part in the flight. This was a once-in-a-lifetime experience for both of us, me as GB and Damian as RAF captain. Many thanks again to Wg Cdr Dean Andrew and Gp Capt Greg Bagwell [my pilot] for making this happen and giving us both such an amazing day.

That day was a building block for the professional and Service games to link up. I have since given various coaching sessions, as have many clubs and coaches, to personnel at RAF Stations while, in return, the professional game, both at club and international level, has benefitted from some brilliant motivational techniques and team-building activities from the RAF, stuff that would not normally be as readily available.

There is a massive mutual respect between the professional game and the Military one. From our perspective how can you not respect what these guys and girls do for our country? No matter how tough we think it is on the field of play, they are out there putting their lives on the line for us.

How tough must it be to know you may have to do that? You cannot help but have maximum respect.

To read about the battle that Damian has gone through to get rugby league played in the RAF was a real eye opener and is truly inspiring stuff, not to mention the personal traumas his family went through during this period.

In many ways it is a *Boy's Own* story of a lad from Brighouse fighting against the hierarchy for the sport he loves and triumphing in true style, building an association without any kit, equipment or access into the successful one that exists today; a key player in the professional game in more ways than one.

Throughout these pages he wins countless battles in what must be the oldest rivalry in sport, against sometimes seemingly insurmountable odds. But it also shows how love, laughter and comradeship can win against even the toughest opponents on a personal level.

The game has always battled for supremacy against the other code and I can see why the structure of something like the RAF - with many of the senior personnel coming from a university background and perhaps wanting to promote the sport they know - would make this even harder.

Having played at the highest level in the game, I feel that rugby league as a spectacle and a sport is second to none. If you ask any rugby union or football fan to attend a match you're sure they'll go away enthused and always want more. They love it and I am not surprised as the product on the field is first class.

It is just such a shame that the sport doesn't get the coverage and acknowledgement that it truly deserves.

It has always been like this, but to see the success and victories Damian and Service rugby league have had is fantastic. I am not surprised, knowing the type of person he is. Once he gets his teeth into something he never lets go.

One thing that always surprises about Damian is his age! He is a big kid at heart... and certainly doesn't look 40-plus! I don't know how much paint he puts on that wig of his, but he doesn't look or act his years.

Historically, it was the Military that helped spread the

word of rugby union to an international audience during various conflicts, and this is another aspect within these pages that shows the importance the modern Military plays in taking the game to corners of the globe it would not normally reach.

I was humbled when I read of the efforts of the RAF Rugby League Association in helping to build the game in Russia, Jamaica and Canada. The stories are a great example of how our wonderful game can cross cultural boundaries and unite people, building great and long-lasting friendships.

This aspect and the continuation of the code's other values; those of discipline, professionalism and respect, not only for your opponents, but officials too, shows the true worth of the Military to our game and that continues year in year out with the tours undertaken by each Service.

In my own role at St Helens RLFC, as ambassador for the club, these values are proudly upheld. It is wonderful to read about this being taken to new parts of the globe and ingrained in younger generations for the future of our game, just as I saw in Damian's young son Connor as he walked out beside me as match mascot for an international clash with New Zealand in 2005.

One aspect of the book that really struck me was the rivalry between the Services, which came across in some of the tough duels between the RAF, Army and Navy, particularly the RAF against the Navy!

In many ways the rivalries are deeper than in the professional game. Well, these guys don't get paid to play. They are doing it for the will to win and it's great to hear stories about these little-known characters of the sport battling with pride for their shirt and colours.

It says something of the man himself that I knew nothing of his battles to install rugby league as one of the major sports in the Military. It must also be said that he has had a big impact on the national team and has a great knowledge of the game. I truly believe the Rugby Football League could make much more use of him in the coming years.

The knowledge, desire and understanding of the game, its history, its relevance and its impact on everyday life that he has, cannot be put into somebody. It is in-built and this book shows how this has helped him win some tough tussles, keeping his belief and pushing on through for the sport he loves.

I am glad the work of Damian and Military rugby league has been put into print and hope it serves to inspire and entertain any prospective or existing sportsmen and women to achieve all they can.

Keep it up mate!

*Paul Sculthorpe, September 2013*

# Gasping for Air

*22 September 2006*

ONE more try should seal it … heat and dust buzzing around my head … difficult to concentrate, but it will be down to one chance.

I've seen enough, played enough to know that.

They are game, but we are in a good place … the team are around me, we are pulling together … that word, THE word, that will mean so much in the future, at the moment in its infancy, but it is flickering MATESHIP … that's what my team has got …

It is flickering and beginning to show itself, the future could be now, just strike out … make the move to seal the win, that's it Clayton, do it …

The ball brakes, my studs struggle to grip on the dusty surface …

'Christ it's hot' …

There, a gap, if I can receive the ball now, there is a real chance.

## Through Adversity

Then bang, I am knocked off line as the game bursts into life again over a short distance, so much movement, so much potential ...

Spider plays the ball wide, I cut inside seeing the gap, hackles up ... bristling, muscles stretch, then it's there, the ball, pupils dilate ... adrenaline rushes, and then a chink of light, their midfield brakes ...

Surely this is it ...

Panting, the sound of calls become crystal clear. Move right, hold that ball tight ... roll a challenge, hands grab at my socks, pulling through, carry this dead weight ... I will lose him soon enough ...

Should I release or hang on? Choose to kick, I stick a bomb up ...

Chasing over the try-line, I'm gonna score, ... dive ...

BANG ...

Muffled sound, almost underwater ... one thought: 'Did I touch the ball? As the Navy full-back and winger collided into me?' ... then I feel the first of the pain, as sound returns ...

I hear my breath, delayed seemingly after the impact ... 'Aaahhhh', my lungs force out the air as I drop to the ground, the contact with terra firma leaves me limp for a second, vision blurs ... bloody dust doesn't help...

Gasping for air now, my hand reaches for my knee, agony, searing pain from inside ... this is bad and I know it ...

This couldn't be any worse ... is my first fear ...

The game moves on for a second ... for some reason I, with a sideways view of the pitch, am trying to work out what the ref has given, then space as the game moves away from me … Get used to it moving away, I tell myself … all that effort and now this …

All that potential and now this … what is this about? How unfair …

A hand rests on my knee, a voice jokes, then laughter, but I am lost …

The back garden …

The first game …

My dad, my team, my love of this sport and all I can hear now is their laughter …

All the meetings, the shitty evenings in the pissing rain … Lorraine … rugby league …

Where would it go now?

Hands help me from the pitch, brain distorted … emotions blurred …

What next?

What next?

What next?

# From Brighouse to Uxbridge

*5 April 1992*

*In rugby league history:* 5 April (1992): In the Stones Bitter Championship (the forerunner of Super League) Bradford Northern beat Wakefield Trinity 9-8; Featherstone Rovers lost to Wigan 13-34; Swinton beat Hull 27-18; Hull KR lost to Leeds 4-13; Widnes beat Salford 24-20.

*In RAF history:* 5 April (1965): In response to a Soviet threat to the air corridors into Berlin, Argosy transport aircraft conducted a series of 10 probing flights into and out of Berlin between 5 and 10 April. On 4 April an RAF Germany fighter squadron deployed to the Luftwaffe airfield at Celle, previously occupied by the RAF between 1945 and 1957, to escort the flights into Berlin, should that prove necessary. In the event, escorts were not required.

I wasn't really bothered about the academic side of life when I was in school, it was always sport for young master Clayton, and that is pretty much how it has remained.

Looking back I never realised, or have since really analysed, how important or integral to my life rugby league, especially Brighouse Rangers Amateur Rugby League Club, was and would become.

It is funny to think about how the skills picked up on the field, within the game itself and the family ethic that is so essential to rugby league would be ingrained in me and unconsciously used throughout my life and RAF career.

I started playing at nine years old, as a scrum-half. My dad always seemed to have played the game and the house always seemed to be busy with the Brighouse U18s side at weekends. Dad was a keen supporter and, of course, my sisters liked the lads being around, so the game just seemed part of the patchwork of our family life. It has stayed that way.

That unity and 'mate-ship' has helped me through some dark times and taught me, in many ways, how to deal with the slings and arrows I suppose.

The first of those arrows was to arrive when I was 11, when my dad, who had worked in the local carpet factory, Firths, where his father had worked and his father's father and so on, was facing redundancy.

The factory, which has since been knocked down, was laying people off and there had been adverts for staff to move over to America to train their workers to use the Axminster looms, which were being shipped to Pennsylvania. Dad applied, got a job and after four years over there had his green card. I remember the plan had been for us to join him, but my mum Janet wanted my older sisters, Rachel and Sarah, to finish their education in England.

It became apparent after a while that things had broken down between my parents and that dad would not be returning home, or us heading out to America. We would not be a family, in the nuclear sense, ever again.

## Through Adversity

For me it was, obviously, a sad time, but my mum set about retaining the family unit. One example of that was never failing to get me to league matches - ensuring I played the sport I loved.

Wherever we were playing, be it Keighley, Leeds, wherever, mum would pack us up in her red Mini and off we'd go.

'If Damian wanted to play rugby league, then he would,' was how mum saw it.

It is funny how the same thing has happened with my wife, Lorraine, and our son Connor. He has never missed a training session at Halifax RLFC or Sheffield Wednesday's Academy. Even though I was away a lot of the time with work, Lorraine got him there.

Our Connor went from being football mad to following his dad's sport, and has over the years proved himself to be a good sportsman, with a great attitude.

He started playing football, funnily enough, thanks to his mum starting up an U11s team. Then after attending a Soccer School in Bradford he was sent for a trial at Leeds United, then Sheffield United, but neither of them picked him up, before Sheffield Wednesday did.

It was one hell of a commitment, what with training three times a week and playing at weekends, but they released him at 14 years old. His grandad, a lifelong Owls fan, was very proud of the time Connor spent there.

My son got his first taste of rugby league when meeting a lot of the Australian players. From there he was bitten, playing for Ovenden, then Calderdale Service Area and from there, in his second year, he was selected for Yorkshire's U18s, aged just 16. He even trialled for England before training with Halifax's U23s, aged 17.

Come hell or high water, my mum, who was a West

Yorkshire lass born in Rastrick, was the same, so in a way life has mirrored that commitment to family and the game.

My mum, who was the daughter of a coalman, lost her mother at a young age. Perhaps that's partly why she supported me so much. That close relationship has come at a price though, the price of ridicule from my sisters, who always comment on mum buying me Classic biscuits when I come home - even to this day. But I can take it.

Slowly Brighouse Rangers became the mainstay of all our friends - my mum's, sisters' and mine - as our family began to heal its wounds.

One of the club's founder members, Jeff Greenwood, in some ways became like a father figure to me - he probably still is. He was always there for me and I still look forward to meeting up with him whenever I return to the club.

Training was Tuesday and Thursday, plus I played for my school on Saturday and then Brighouse on a Sunday.

I lived for it.

My first boots were Mitre football boots and my first set of screw-in stud boots were Puma. I loved them.

I then got a pair of hand-me-down Adidas Flankers. They were too big for me. I'd never had a pair of Adidas in my life, well not ones with three stripes on anyway. Mine always had a few more stripes!

The older lads at Brighouse gave them to me. I had size six feet and these were size eight, so I padded out the toes. I thought they were amazing and wanted to wear them, I just got around the obvious size difference.

I cleaned them religiously, using a nailbrush and bucket of water outside sat on the step. I took all the studs out and made sure they were spot on.

Putting dubbing on, I made a special point of wiping it off the yellow Adidas stripes. That attention to detail manifests itself in my recent role as the Station Warrant Officer at RAF Cranwell.

I remember the excitement when my mate Chris Senior and I hooked up during the school week and weekends. It was rugby league full throttle. Chris, who lived in Whinney Hill, played stand-off and I scrum-half. We would practise plays and moves in the street at night, jumpers for goal posts type stuff, until it got dark or mum called us in.

St Andrew's Junior was a school of about 300 kids, and it was at the time of the 11-plus examination. The choice was either take it and pass, ensuring a better education at a grammar school, or face going to a Secondary Modern, with the choice of Eastfield, which I didn't see as good.

Our Saturdays would be spent watching the 1st or 2nd team at Brighouse. We would be all over the place, getting balls if they went out of the ground or into the stream that ran adjacent to the pitch.

Having practised all week I would be up on a Sunday morning, Chris would come round, we would walk down at about 8.30am, talking about what we would do during the mile-long walk to the club; getting more excited as we walked down Bracken Road, along Bradford Road to Welholme Park, home of Brighouse Rangers ARLFC.

There was no glamour at Brighouse, we bathed in large sinks, no showers, holes in the ceiling, nails for hangers, but we thought it was brilliant. The pitch was very small, on a slight slope with a massive dip in one corner, meaning in the winter it was a mud bath, but above all else it was ours - the Rangers' home turf and one which the opposition did not enjoy visiting. The camaraderie was excellent and because I was one of the smallest and youngest with a lot of promise, I was taken in by the bigger lads.

I never got beat up at school, I gained a little bit more respect, because of my ability of being able to play rugby league and being at the club. It helped me a lot, especially as a skinny lad.

I was like the runt in many of the team pictures, but other lads at school and in the surrounding area left me well alone due to my friends.

My sort of heroes, or players I respected, were all amateur, which is probably unusual now. There was a guy called Nigel Marshall. He was five years older than me, scrum-half at Brighouse, lots of talent. He eventually turned professional for Halifax. I remember being 12 and he would let me train with him, always going out of his way to speak to me. I thought that was fantastic.

I saw him play Queensbury RL and there was a 26-man brawl. One of their players took him out, which sparked the incident, and the crowd joined in. I recall one guy wading in with his crash helmet. I was terrified on the touchline.

There was another guy, Paul Nuttall, who went out with my sister. I remember we would go most weekends during the close season to his house with a couple of balls. He lived about a mile from my mum's and we would practise kicking all the time.

I'd be kicking goals for hours, he was brilliant with me. He was 18 and yet he would spend hours practising and teaching me, a kid. It got to the point where I could kick the ball from the try line, curl the ball in and bounce it in off the back post.

This sort of thing just built my love for the game. When I was old enough the lads and Paul took me to see Bradford Northern (nowadays Bulls) every Sunday, which was a brilliant adventure.

There I was with all the older lads, out on the bus. I

remember mum would pack me off with my fare and enough to get me into the ground. It was an amazing time for a rugby league-mad lad.

It was all so different at school though.

Having passed my 11-plus I was in at Hipperholme Grammar School for Boys. Situated on the outskirts of Halifax, the school had about 400 pupils and during our first physical education lesson I discovered that the place only played cricket, hockey and rugby union.

When our teacher Trevor Liddington, smelly Trev we nicknamed him, got us all together to practise scoring tries, he gave the ball to one lad called Paul Walsh, who also joined the RAF as a MTD, and was a union lad.

Walsh fannied about for a bit then touched the ball under the posts. Liddington reluctantly gave the ball to me after I'd announced I played for Brighouse Rangers.

I ran the 15 yards to the try line and dived over into all this mud. Liddington turned to the others and said: 'Now that's how to score a try'. He later wrote in my annual report: 'Clayton is the best prospect at scrum-half this school has seen in a decade'.

But it wasn't rugby league was it?

I also dabbled in playing cricket, at wicketkeeper. No point standing out on the boundary is there? I only played cricket because it meant avoiding lessons.

Hipperholme was supposed to be my chance of a better education, but I had no real time for that coming away with just two O'Levels in English and Art before spending a year at Brighouse Girls Grammar school. But to be honest I simply spent the year there talking to the girls and did not add to my examination tally.

Brighouse had sides for all age groups, but there is obviously a time when you realise that your dream of being a professional rugby league star is not going to happen and so it was for me. When I left school I was faced with the reality of working life.

I remember walking up those steps into the Bradford RAF careers office. I had no idea what I wanted to be; I was literally a 17-year-old lad out in Bradford who just walked in there to see what sort of trades were on offer.

I had no idea I wanted to be in the Service and when they mentioned the driving job [Military Transport], I said 'Yes', simply because I thought they would pay for my driving lessons.

I didn't realise that they did that for most other trades too. With hindsight I could have applied for many other careers.

I am not sure whether dad's departure had in some ways driven me towards a life in the Service, the family role and unity it could provide? I knew I wasn't happy with where I was and didn't want to work in a factory.

I clearly remember recognising the head of the family role when I was 15, 16 years old, so maybe I was looking for that in reverse from the RAF, as I had experienced similar from Brighouse previously? I also just knew at the time my life was going nowhere.

So four months shy of my 18th birthday I was signed up and sent to RAF Swinderby, which doesn't exist now, near Lincoln, to begin my seven weeks basic training and sport would be part of that. I never thought for a minute that rugby league would not be played in the Service. Why would I?

It was 1987 and it was just a game like any other, one of the big five. Add to that the fact that we were in Lincoln, not far from the North.

Swinderby was at the time what RAF Halton is today, home of basic training for the non-commissioned ranks.

## Through Adversity

I remember being asked by the PTI if I played rugby. I said: 'Of course, rugby league, scrum-half.' To which the reply was: 'Well, you will be able to catch a ball at least.'

In a small way things began to dawn on me when we could only take part in rugby union games during training. I did think at the time they may have only played the one code due to logistics and so on.

I clearly recall turning out for 14 Flight and there was this Welsh lad there.

Because of his nationality, it was presumed he would be good at rugby, dyed in the wool and all that.

Well, me and some other Northern lads smashed him in the game, but despite this we were still overlooked, due to the rugby league roots we had. I did not let it bother me.

I had no real idea what to expect from the training. Being 17, with no drinking allowed, socialising was restricted and normal life broken due to bunking up in an 18-man room, it was really unusual. We were woken up at 5.30am with bed inspections and I thought I would be clever and suss the system out after making up my locker by putting the key for it in my bed pack, so it was handy.

During the inspection my pack was thrown across the room, which was normal for whoever was being singled out, and the key, of course, fell out, which led to my locker being tipped out. That taught me for being cute.

Cpl Mike Sweeney was the bloke doing the chucking and I recall him bawling me out to tidy up my room as the others went on parade. I met him about 10 years later and outranked him, which was quite funny.

We undertook GST (General Service Training), which included rifle drills and range firing. It also helped with the transition into Service life and introduced us to ceremonial drill and deportment.

That was followed by GDT (General Defence Training), which saw things get a little bit tougher with respirator drills, where they made you take off your respirator while in a chamber full of smoke and CS gas. You are then told to recite name, rank and number, while choking in the CS and Christ it makes your eyes sting, I can tell you.

We got a right 'beasting' on a three-day training camp in RAF North Luffenum, in Rutland, which, like many RAF Stations, is no longer there. The RAF Regiment guys did a lot of things like the 'Respirator Run', but, although they wouldn't get away with it now, it really did and does bond you together as trainees.

I met LAC Dave Mortimer while I was there. Little did either of us know the impact he would have on me 10 years later. At that time he just ignored me.

I had a great time in basic training, had a right laugh, met some great lads and it seemed obvious to this Brighouse lad that I was set for this RAF malarkey, no dramas.

The sporting divide reared its head again, during my eight-week Phase Two training at RAF St Athan, Wales, which featured more of the same. I finally 'passed out' while I was there and that was a really proud moment with my grandad, John Willy Rastrick, there to see me.

I just wanted to get my training done to be honest. I acquired my LGV driving licence and finally said goodbye to Gus Boden, with whom I had signed on and gone through training.

He was posted to Halton and I dropped him off there before heading to Uxbridge. He has now left the RAF after 20 years service.

So there I was, LAC Clayton, posted to RAF Uxbridge - which has just recently closed - that became the home of RAF rugby league for 15 years.

## Through Adversity

Synonymous with the Battle of Britain, Uxbridge housed the famous 'bunker' from which the air defence of England against the German Luftwaffe in the Second World War was planned and then monitored.

It became a home to me in July 1987. If I am honest, I didn't really know where it was, 'down South' and so on, but it marked the start of some huge moments in my life.

The Station itself was just on the outskirts of town. It was a relatively large Station given its locality and played home to several sports, including football and us.

A Spitfire overlooked the main parade square and I had some good times there, using all my contacts to enable us to return with the RAF Rugby League Association several years after I had originally arrived.

My job entailed any logistical transportation from the Central Band of the Royal Air Force to, well, anything that was needed.

Life at the Station was good. We were put in single-man rooms, although the state of the accommodation did upset my mum when she came to visit me, she thought it was so bad.

I made good pals with John Gomez, Justin Dando, Jock Cousins and the now FS Lynne Prince, with Lynne and myself being the only two left in the Service - she is at Halton nowadays.

My working life saw me hook up with my new MT boss WO Chris Wren, great name and a great bloke. He is the gospel on anything to do with the Battle of Britain and is the curator of the bunker or Ops Room at Uxbridge.

He had us constantly lugging stuff up and down the steps for him. He drove us mad, much the same way I do now with the young lads who work under me when it comes to rugby league things.

Wren was a good boss and was one of the first to call me 'Clakka', which is my widely known nickname in the Service.

Once I had settled down I began looking around for some rugby to play and, of course, there was always going to be Station matches.

I remember signing up and being told it was union only. I was shocked, but I had experienced this before when I was at Hipperholme. So for me Sunday would still be rugby league day and that would entail plenty of driving about in later years.

I was still playing for Brighouse at weekends, driving home to play, with my petrol being paid for by the club.

It was just something I was prepared to do for the sport I love and, thankfully, I had someone who understood my passion for the sport and supported me all the way, Lorraine.

That support began on a blind date on New Year's Eve 1988 in Halifax. My then best friend, Craig Blackburn, had invited me out to Elland all trussed up in fancy dress. He was going out with Lorraine's best mate at the time and we all hooked up.

Lorraine was dressed as a harlequin, so I didn't get to see what she really looked like, while I was done up as a pirate, with the earrings and so on. I looked a right tit, but we got on like a house on fire, despite the costumes and she was a Halifax lass so all was well in the world.

I was enjoying my Service life and my rugby league games, which saw me returning home most weekends, this kept my love of league going. I was buzzing from the games.

Originally it was a double bonus for me, I was returning home to play and see my girlfriend, who loved rugby league. That shared love has gone a long way to keeping things going for us. We were very happy and when Lorraine moved down to Uxbridge in May 1990, we got married in the September. Life seemed to click into place; emotionally, Service wise and in the world of rugby league.

The real turning point for me in the Service was when a civilian guy called Steve Bowers, who worked at MoD Main Building in Whitehall, London, sent out an entry in SROs [Station Routine Orders] across the RAF, enquiring about interest in rugby league.

That was in 1992 and I remember discussing this with Lorraine, how it would cut out the mileage and how life could become more settled.

Neither of us could have known how much that SRO and the consequent inaugural meeting of the RAFRLA, held at RAF Benson on Sunday, 5 April 1992, would change our lives forever.

# Rustling Feathers

*11 May 1994*

*In rugby league history: On 12 May (1937): Coronation Day, Leeds played an exhibition game against Salford with 12-a-side, with the loose forward being taken out, Leeds won 15-9.*

*In RAF history: 11 May (1944): The air campaign against enemy airfields within 150 miles of the Normandy invasion beaches was intensified. The land offensive in Italy began to break the Gustav line and finally capture Monte Cassino. Medium bombers attacked road and rail communications and fighter bombers provided direct support for ground forces.*

I FIND it funny to think of that young SAC, as I was then, learning to play the Service's game just to play the game I loved so much. That is the only way things can be achieved in the Military and I was shrewd enough and lucky enough, career position wise, to be able to use this to my advantage, as far as rugby league was concerned at least.

## Through Adversity

Having read Bowers' SRO, the least athletic man I have ever seen involved in rugby league, I remember going back to talk to my staunchest team-mate, Lorraine, about what 'we' should do. At that time I was only playing league at weekends in Halifax and union during the week.

The opportunity to play closer to home, probably leave the union side of things behind and, of course, be at the start of building something for the game should have been enough incentive for me to snatch Bowers' hand off.

But I was umming and arring, while Lorraine was saying: 'Oh just go down there. What have you got to lose?'

In those early days Lorraine was my main motivator, she would always say: 'Get amongst it Damian, stop fannying about and go for it,' which is exactly what I needed.

She was right. Then again, she usually is.

RAF Benson was only 50 minutes away from Uxbridge and that was the venue for the initial meeting/trial on 5 April 1992. So we both packed off for the Saturday morning trip to the Station in our old Vauxhall Cavalier, complete with spoiler kit and all. It was lovely that car.

What I arrived to see was in many ways like the fabulous five, only in numbers - that was how many turned up. There was a trial practice, before Bowers held a meeting to organise some sort of informal committee, during which I was selected as secretary. It was always Ragtail Rovers at the start, but we knew the importance of being as professional as possible. We had no kit, no pitch, balls nor anything to speak of really, but we could get a committee together to start things rolling, so that's what we did.

It was here that my positioning, job role, placement or whatever you want to call it, began to prove so invaluable. I was driving a 2-star, Major General Roy Wood, at the time. He was, and still is, a great guy, very supportive of what I was doing and my career and always wanted to chat about stuff. He seemed to look on me as a sort of surrogate son.

An orienteer by sport, I would talk ideas with him while driving up and down the country in his Service issue Rover Montego. He would always ask what I had been up to and I clearly recall mentioning the meeting and my new role as secretary. Immediately he suggested that I should run my draft minutes and administration past his PA, meaning all my correspondence was backed up by his office and compiled in Service writing.

It was fabulous. There I was a young SAC with the full support of his 'own' outer office.

I knew the value of this, having met a guy called Tom O'Donovan, who was the sport's National Development Executive. He had been looking to expand the sport in the Forces, but he did not fully understand the workings of Service life and the hierarchical structure of it.

During the War years there were two codes, but the playing of rugby league was not allowed, meaning legends such as Alex Murphy had to play union for the RAF. There were only a couple of rugby league matches played, the first being when the league lads played the England rugby union team in a one-off match and beat them. That match was entitled Northern Command, when a union XV play a league XV at Headingley on Saturday, January 23, 1943, KO 3.30pm. The posters advertising it stated: 'Every player a star. Come and settle those arguments - Once and for all.' The result of the game, played under union rules, was 18-11 to the league side. The second match was played at the Odsal Stadium, Bradford, on Saturday, April 29, 1944, and ended with a score of 15-10 to the league team.

So O'Donovan knew that history would need to be repeated if the sport was to grow, but his efforts, asking questions in the Houses of Parliament, pressuring the RAF Sports board and Tri-Service sports board, just seemed to cause consternation. He managed just a few games, one of which was against the Fusiliers at St Helens RLFC ground, Knowsley Road, before it all fell flat.

To get the gist of how many feathers O'Donovan had ruffled, I remember receiving a call from AVM Bob Honey, then Director of the RAF Sports Board, asking about RAF Marham's refusal [See Hansard entry from House of Commons dated June 2, 1992, below] to allow a rugby league tournament to be played on the Station, with the point later being raised in the House.

More importantly, he had lit the necessary fires.

## House of Commons, Tuesday, 2 June, 1992

## The House met at 2.30pm [Madam Speaker in the Chair] Oral Answers to Questions DEFENCE Sport

**7. Mr. [David] Hinchliffe:** To ask the Secretary of State for Defence if he has any proposals to amend the list of sporting activities recognised within the Armed Forces.

**Mr. Archie Hamilton:** We have no plans at present to alter the list of sports which are officially recognised. The range of sports which enjoy official recognition is, however, kept under review to ensure that it reflects demand originating from grass roots level within the Services.

**Mr. Hinchliffe:** The Minister will recall meeting an all-party delegation in March about the recognition of rugby league in the Armed Forces. What steps were taken to communicate the outcome of that meeting to the heads of establishments and units within the Armed Forces? Why, at certain RAF stations, were station orders posted indicating that personnel should not have contact with the RFL's national development officer? Why were personnel at RAF Marham, who were organising a rugby league competition next Saturday, refused permission to use the pitches at that base? That seems to be completely against the spirit of what was agreed at the meeting in March.

**Mr. Hamilton:** As I assured the Hon. Gentleman at the meeting, we were happy to give him all possible facilities in terms of publicity material which would be circulated within the three Armed Services. I have no idea why facilities should have been debarred or such notices put up: it is totally against the spirit of the undertaking that I gave the Hon. Gentleman at our meeting, and I will investigate both events.

To think that something like that had worked its way down the chain of command to a young SAC, from the House, is amazing really.

What it really meant, if you pick the bones out of it, was that the game had been pretty much ostracised in the Service. We needed nothing that the union guys didn't use, same kit, balls etcetera really, but no, we weren't allowed to play. Simple: no room at the inn.

After our initial meeting, we indirectly became the tool for the RFL to push rugby league in the Service. It seems a bit wild to think that now we were just a bunch of enthusiasts scratching around trying to find 17 blokes who wanted to play rugby league. We had one hell of a fight on our hands, but I was learning how to duck and dive all the time. We were slowly picking up the numbers, had a better level of support from voices in authority and we had a momentum, slight at first, but momentum nonetheless.

The first major step came during a meeting at Adastral House in London with Gp Capt (Ret'd) Maurice Short of the RAF Sports Board. He was, and always has been, a top man. He gave me the nod to use official Service mail during that meeting; to grant me something like that was incredibly useful.

I remember him regaling anyone who would listen with the facts of that initial meeting, when I invited him to attend an Inter-Services match a few years back, telling everyone about this young SAC turning up at his office.

So from my first interaction with him I had managed to get him onside, but I knew I had to do things the way he wanted. He knew the ins and outs and I wanted to learn how to do things properly. My mindset was not to get knocked back all the time. I would always pop in and see him whenever I was in London, always try and listen, always be upbeat, you know, be a pain in the ass really, so he would say 'yes' to get rid of me.

Although, in their eyes, it was the less attractive and desirable game, the working class game, I never had any hostility from those important Service people. They just saw me as an enthusiastic young man with a passion and I think in plain and simple language, that they were good men. My willingness to learn and quick thinking enabled me to build the foundations of a successful career and there I was selected for promotion to Warrant Officer, at 38, one of the youngest in my trade's and Service history, so I think I learned well.

The role of secretary has developed over the years it has to be said; in the first place it was really just me acting as a conduit between the various parties such as the sports board, the hierarchy, players and venues.

There were three of us doing the administrative side of things. I was also concentrating on playing which, to be honest, was far more important to me at that time. So I was secretary, Ian Calvert was treasurer and Steve Bowers was generally helping to attract players to the new association through SROs.

Our first task was to raise interest in the sport and raise the profile of the association. During one of my first meetings with Short he said: 'It's going to be a struggle for you guys.' So that was a good starting point, I thought.

Tom O'Donovan had compiled a database of 200-plus names in the Service who were interested in the sport, so I began compiling letters and sending them out to each name on the list. As we gained momentum we persuaded Wg Cdr Adrian Sumner to become our chairman and I was learning from the Sports Board, while writing letters, designing and sending out invites, as well as designing our kit and trying to gain sponsorship.

I was master of all trades you could say, wearing a lot of different hats. The modern role is purely secretarial, as other work is delegated, we didn't have that luxury back then.

Once we had achieved things such as official Military mail, the 10-foot wall, the other things we found ourselves facing seemed like five-foot walls. From there, another team trial at Marham saw 20 players turn up, along with Lorraine and me. I clearly remember her knitting in the car while we played and then questioning me afterwards, saying: 'Damo, who was that big fella?' after being amazed at the pace and power of a player creating hell on the pitch.

It was Tony Holmes, a tough and skilful player from Hull. JT at the time, now a civilian working for Turners at RAF Coningsby, he would become our first team captain.

Tony and a guy called Al Prout, a young SAC who

also worked for MT like me, and lived about 100-metres away at Uxbridge, were the outstanding players on show, soon to be our building blocks. As far as Al was concerned it was amazing that our paths had never crossed before. We are now best mates and have been since that day. Connor calls him Uncle Al, so that gives you some idea.

He left the Service because his asthma was so bad. It was a tragedy really as nowadays it would have been sorted, but back then it wasn't and he ended up working on the skips for a while - the crafty cockney binman! It's great that we can look back on that sort of thing. It's like a continuum, friends, family, colleagues, all as a result of the game.

One memorable Prout incident came when we were playing 34 Sqn RAF Regiment at RAF Leeming back in 1994. It was going to be, and was, a tough game against that lot. There was a crowd six-deep around the pitch and we were winning. Prout kept fiddling with his shirt during the game, trying to remove his shoulder pads. He eventually took his shirt off and just as he did one of their guys broke through and was running for the try-line so Al, shirtless, ran over and took him out with a massive hit. The crowd went mad.

It was like a wrestling match.

He began coughing up blood after the tackle and was eventually taken to Northallerton Hospital, where he was kept in overnight. The next day Stevie Bowers suggested we went to get him, but they wouldn't let him out. So Steve suggested we grab some breakfast. Bear in mind Bowers is a 20 stone hulk of a man. He had this massive breakfast with a side order of chips. It was 8am and he had this massive plate of food, it sticks in the memory.

The RFL were pushing hard to get us recognised and as organised as possible and they set up a match against the French Army, who had professional players in their ranks.

It was a run-before-we-could-walk situation. The match was to be played at RAF Finningley in Doncaster on 8 October 1992, where I first met Jack Wilson and Wg Cdr Adrian Sumner, who I later persuaded to be our first chairman.

We played a couple of warm-up games for the French fixture, the first against Norfolk Stags, adjacent to RAF Swanton Morley, Norfolk, and the second against Oulton ARLFC, near Dewsbury, borrowing a union kit from RAF Coningsby. It was red and so were our faces after the hammering, just five days before facing the French. Short had told me that we could not use the RAF representative name, because we were not a recognised sport in the Service.

That would be another fight we would face, but for the moment we were named - well, Lorraine and I came up with it one night - the Blue Bombers.

The Blue Bombers playing in red, blimey.

No kit, not much of an idea about tactics, no physiotherapy support, having to pay our own petrol, no time off granted to play and we got torn apart to boot. But we had played and been welcomed by the Oulton guys.

The reaction afterwards was one of elation and things would begin to gather pace very quickly after that first whistle was blown. It was a real against-all-odds moment. Lorraine stood on the side of the pitch in the pouring rain with my mum, always supporting me.

It was a great day for me as well. We were really a young couple enjoying ourselves and the sport we loved.

We had been married a few years and we just did everything together. But all this seemed a long way from chatting on our honeymoon in Blackpool in September 1990, which had been forced on us due to my passport being taken away under orders for Op BOLTON.

## Through Adversity

The Operation saw all Service personnel's passports taken away at the start of the first Gulf War, due to a 48-hour standby being enforced.

The next few years would really see us move on as a couple and, as a family, with the arrival of Connor.

The association was getting vital support from the RFL with things such as insurance and the RAF Sports Board eventually classed us as 'on-duty' during games. Mend and make do, that could be a catchphrase for me in a lot of ways.

I remember when we received our first kit, donated by the RFL. I had to drive to Chapeltown in Leeds on the day of the French Army match.

Chapeltown is an area of Leeds that is famous for its nightlife, well ladies of the night, shall we say. I am not sure if there is something in that or not? It's always puzzled me.

Picking up the kit reminded me of the Christmas I was given a Manchester United top by my mum. The other lads in my area, such as Chris Senior, had the proper Admiral kit. Mine had Admiralty written on it. To be fair, the other lads said nothing, we just went out in them and I was delighted.

It was the same with the first RAF kit, all blue with dark blue designs on it, including an eagle and rugby ball. I was as chuffed then as I was with the Admiralty kit.

I had always tried to make the best of things, but now I had a group of lads who were doing the same, none of us batted an eyelid, we were up and running.

The kit showed how important we were to the RFL. It was great and I don't know many sports whose governing body would go as far as that to help a side, and a ragtail one at that. The support went all the way. The referee of the game was a legend called Fred Lindop and the chairman of the RFL, Bob Ashby, came to watch.

My keen eye for an opportunity really showed itself

when Ashby spoke at the aftermatch dinner and said: 'You've represented your country today lads, you will all be getting a Great Britain tie.' Well you can imagine the reaction. There I was writing a letter on the Monday asking where the ties were? I've still got mine.

Ashby also said that we would be going to play a return match in Fontainebleau, France, paid for by the RFL, against the Army. I remember adding in the letter: 'We would like to take you up on your generous offer of the match in France'. I was learning fast.

We were now tying in with the Army, who had two main players, Major Martin Morris and Cpl Martin Coyd. I went on to become great friends with Coyd.

He was really me on the Army side and it has always been a source of personal upset for me when I was rewarded for my services to the game and Coydy wasn't. We had done it together really and I remember his voice when I called to tell him I had been awarded an MBE. He was delighted, but his pride was hurt. It was tough for me to take as he is a great bloke and it was an injustice really. He should have gained that recognition too.

So the year proved a landmark one. I had also been promoted to Corporal, based back at Uxbridge, where I was working for AVM John Feesey out of Civil Aviation Authority House in Kingsway, London.

My new boss then became the President of our association after a few conversations with the evermore-convincing Clayton. He was a great bloke and said 'Yes' straight away and supported me brilliantly. We are still in touch.

To kick-start the year, there was the inaugural fixture against the Army, which was held at Hilton Park, Leigh - home of Leigh RLFC - played on 11 May 1994. The best arrival of all came along when Connor James Clayton was born in Hillingdon Hospital on January 31. It was a fantastic time for both of us.

My wife being my wife didn't rest on her laurels, we still went up and down to the North. Our friendships bloomed in Uxbridge and, while I was working, I had gained my own personal secretary after she gave up working at an insurance brokers in Watford.

I used to bounce ideas off her all the time. She designed letterheads for us and we would talk through kit designs and so on. She gave me the benefit of her opinion and I clearly remember returning home from work most nights to find dozens of notes stuck all over the fridge or the kitchen windows, listing all the calls she had taken.

I would get in at 8pm and chat with Connor in his high chair, while she 'debriefed' me on who called and what was going on. It was amazing really and drew us closer and closer together as a result.

That would bode well when we came to deal with the tougher times that lay ahead.

Things really gained ground when the *Daily Telegraph* reported on our first match under the new guise. We played the Civil Service, won comfortably and the headline said: 'Mudlarks make merry as RAF ground Civil Service to a halt'.

We now had our own coach in the shape of Jack Wilson, paid for by the RFL.

He came to Uxbridge, where Lorraine and I put him up. It was an amazing time and great to be involved in. Teams were popping up all over ... one in Bruggen, Germany, the Uxbridge Blues, RAF Regt 34 Sqn at Leeming, RAF Coningsby - it was fabulous and growing bigger and better.

Lorraine was integral to the whole thing. We never had that, 'I'm off to play rugby, see you later love' situation.

It was always 'where are WE going to play rugby the weekend?' And all this while we were knee-deep in nappies. What an amazing woman.

It wasn't all wine and roses though on the sporting side of things.

There would be one major stumbling block in the shape of us gaining official status from the Armed Services Minister, Jeremy Handley.

Having made the announcement to the House, the one thing that was missing was the knowledge that us lot in the RAF couldn't gain recognised status, because of the Service having too many sports and needing to replace one with the other.

To be fair, this is still the way today and guys such as Gp Capt Short had been brilliant with us, and helped as much as they could. It was just protocol.

We were still being pressed to prove that the sport was sustainable at Unit level and sufficient interest existed for 'our' game.

We could see the first line in the sand, but we had to wait a further two years to get across it.

In truth … it didn't stop us, not one bit - it served to drive us on.

# In On the Ground

*1 January 1996*

*In rugby league history:* 1 January (1996): Bradford lost to Halifax 18-22; Castleford lost to Sheffield 12-42; St Helens lost to Leeds 14-20; Warrington lost to Wigan 12-41 (all the home sides lost).

*In RAF history:* 1 January (1927): ACM Sir Hugh Trenchard was created as the first Marshal of the Royal Air Force (MRAF).

IT really was a moment when I found myself looking in from the outside as I, Damian Clayton, MT Driver and Corporal, 24, sat at a dinner with an all-party group of 30 MPs in the House of Commons on 15 May, 1996, giving them the word on rugby league from the shop floor, as it were, in the RAF.

We were invited to attend the dinner with Tom O'Donovan by the then MP for Wakefield David Hinchliffe, in the presence of the late Lord Geoffrey Lofthouse, who chaired the meeting. I clearly remember Army league man Martin Coyd and myself had already acknowledged we were simply acting as tools for the official body of rugby league, but we knew it was helping Service sport and in many ways it was a day that really helped me.

We were to give a presentation on how things were going since we had gained official status. Well, as we knew, for us in the RAF nothing had changed, but for me personally that moment let me know it had.

I understood the magnitude of the event, seeing the portcullis on the napkins and so on, microphones hanging down from the ceiling, and I thrived on it.

I knew we were making a difference. I found it infectious and I grew in confidence during the lunch. From that day onwards I have always used it as a touchstone.

It is known as self-actualisation in the Service, as stated by Maslow (Abraham Maslow: *Hierarchy of Needs. A Theory of Motivation.* 1943), which I used to teach to new SNCOs in Halton. As Maslow states, I did feel I was 'achieving my true worth' and it was fabulous. It is not meant to sound conceited. There was I, a Corporal, speaking out and proving myself.

It had all moved so quickly, from a meeting at Benson, to playing in a borrowed kit against Oulton, to speaking in the House. It was surreal.

I found myself thriving in the position. I had the information that these people wanted and I could interact with them on even terms and, of course, I could help the sport I loved and the people whom I played alongside.

In the Service, rank is endemic but, through the sport, such hierarchy was being circumnavigated and I was now part of that move.

This was a chance to change the historical stance of the Establishment. It was amazing and I was in at ground level. It gave me the confidence and I began to realise that I could engage at a different level of life. I was getting the right results and it was ticking the boxes for me, lighting the fires within. I had learned all this from years before, from dad not being there, to going to the posh schools that didn't recognise us as a sport.

Looking back now I understand this. At the time I didn't, I just wanted to do my best for everyone.

I had got more acquainted with the sporting apartheid of the two disciplines and I was managing to change it, and this was one of the landmark moments. I knew as I was giving the presentation, our leverage would be far greater from then on. I also knew that I had a massive part to play. I was wise enough to learn the importance of it and how to help get what we, as a sport, needed.

In many ways the lunch at the House was also to say thank you for the MPs' help. I suppose nowadays we would have given them a shirt, but we had sod all back then, so we took a meal off them instead.

Thinking about it now, though, we could have given them a Blue Bombers shirt, because they were now redundant. We had become RAF Rugby League.

Attending with Coyd was just. I had teamed up with him a few years before, when we first played the Army at Hilton Park in Leigh, in April 1994. Our passion for the sport shone through. We struck a chord basically and began taking things forward. We were on the phone all the time from then on, all our spare time was taken up with it.

Our situations were different though, because the Army had got the full ticket when it was recognised.

Within the first few months of gaining recognition the RAF began playing a series of matches against good opposition, including Customs and Excise in 1993, Wakefield Police in February 1994 and Midlands Police in Birmingham in the April, raising the standard all the time. In the Midlands game Alex Killen, a big lad, a prop from Widnes, played. It took place in Edgbaston, the Police were a big outfit and bear in mind we had no training sessions, just simply donned the Bombers kit. I walked past Killen before kick-off and he was strapping his hand up really tight. I asked him if he was 'OK'?, he said 'yeah' and carried on binding his arm.

The match was officiated by professional referee Bob Connolly, who was well regarded in the game, and Killen had a blinder, plenty of heavy tackling. So you can imagine my face when he ran past us after the game and told us he was heading off to the hospital.

He had taken his cast, which had been fitted for a broken arm, off. He said: 'I knew you wouldn't let me play with it on and it wouldn't have got past the eyes of the official,' so he cut it off to play the match.

Such was his determination to play for us.

So knowing this sort of thing was going on, knowing what the lads were willing to go through and knowing we, as an association, were getting the right feedback but not getting any further, it was a frustrating time, but we were building.

May 11 proved another big moment, as it was the first time we played the British Army, the icing on the cake. We were roundly welcomed into the rugby league fraternity. I played scrum-half and recall it also being a time of writing letters and tons of organisation.

'It's my pleasure on behalf of the RAF Rugby League Association' was how all the invitational letters started and I clearly remember writing to Gp Capt Short.

Dealing with the RAF Sports Board has a certain symmetry. It has its own wrangles, its own inner workings that must be adhered to and understood. That's fair play, I totally agree, but I had to learn it all, so I did.

## Through Adversity

For any sport or association to be 'recognised' it has to be one of the 40 or so sports that the Board agrees to, and then you can gain public funding. As there are always a certain amount of sports, you have to wait for one that does not garner the right amount of interest - be it from players or just within the Service itself - to drop out. Until then, you are left on the periphery.

Being outside the loop means life is hard, really hard in some ways. Your players are expected to give so much more and the association has a much tougher job.

To gain recognised status you have to prove you have enough interest. This is the rule across all three Services, but we could not be added to the RAF's list of recognised sports, so as a fast-growing sport it was agreed that we should come under the one umbrella of rugby, with league and union below that.

It worked and it meant we gained the much-coveted Travel Authority.

We were given Duty Status which means, in layman's terms, if a player is injured, under the mechanics of the Service, they would help with rehabilitation and subsequent compensation, if required.

The association has always done its own accounts. We produce a 'five-year' plan which we present to the Sports Board. It deals with things like kit and any equipment needed and comes from the Sports Lottery. Then there is the Ops Costs, which we bid for. This is the day-to-day costs of the association such as postage, medical support and insurance - the basics.

For us in the early days, I was on the phone all the time to the Sports Board. But it is now more a case of guidance to ensure we are doing the right thing. In many cases we are seen as an example for other associations, such as our Grand Final trophy guard work, which is a great coup for us and shows others how they can be involved at the highest level of their sports.

I know the Sports Board have waxed lyrical about us in the past and for some this is a bitter pill to swallow. They want us to fail. But, to give one example, we have helped the football guys raise their game with the presentation of their matches and it is a pleasure to work with such top blokes who are simply trying to better their sport in the Service - and what a job they are doing now.

For the Army game, Leigh RLFC were enthusiastic and they invited us to play at their ground at no cost.

Shaun Hainsworth won man of the match and Phil Clarke, former Great Britain and Wigan star and Sky Sports presenter, gave him the trophy. We had people from Wigan come, professional players attending a match like that. Can you imagine what that felt like? We were made to feel vital to the whole family of rugby league, despite losing 26-22.

Personally I didn't recognise how big the whole thing was to the RFL. You get some idea now when you put dots on the landscape where the sport was played. Basically the M62 corridor and Cumbria is where the game is strongest. The Student teams take it a little further, but when you look at where the Service plays it takes the sport national. We were pushing that forward.

I did not realise this at the time, but having been involved at boardroom level I began to understand, although at the time most of my efforts were involved in organising sponsorship and advertising for the match. My dealings with Isostar, a sports drink company, proved one of the more memorable.

In the league trade press they were doing some sort of promotion, where you got a drinks bucket and 18 bottles or some such of Isostar, so I wrote to them and asked if we could take advantage of the scheme.

It was a right faff. I had to go into Dewsbury and pick this stuff up the day before the game.

I wanted us to look as professional as possible, but to get the drinks for nothing I was expected to put up banners at the game. 'Fair enough,' I thought.

So between speaking to everyone, holding a meeting with Coydy and so on, I am talking to the groundsman and going round the ground tacking up these bloody Isostar banners on the pitchside hoardings.

I have actually got a picture somewhere of me running around like a tit with these big banners. Nothing has changed before matches today. I always seem to be doing that sort of thing, and it makes me laugh looking back.

In the game I played opposite a guy called Andy Sangar, with whom I went on to play Combined Services rugby league.

He has coached the Army first team in both disciplines, funny how many of the original faces are still showing their worth in the Services game nowadays.

It shows that we were worth our salt and it was worth fighting for from the start.

If the lads thought that playing on a professional ground like Leigh was something to remember, the invite from the King of Morocco was something to definitely make a song and dance about. It came later in the year, and we went out as a Joint Services team. Major Morris did the groundwork for it and then selected a team.

We played the Moroccan national side and Great Britain Students, in a week-long event. It really was amazing just as an adventure, but the goodwill for the sport really built a unity between the two Services. It was a great milestone.

For me I found myself double-taking. Family life was taking off, although it was never a question with Lorraine about rugby fitting in. With matches, tours or anything, she was practically packing me onto the plane.

How good is that? And my career was blooming; all was good in camp Clayton.

If I think back now my career in the sport and my family life, especially that of my son Connor, things ran simultaneously. He was taking his first steps as we were as an association, funny how life works. He has grown as I have, and as the sport in the Service has.

Back at the coalface, we were representing the RAF, even though certain sections of the Service didn't want us to. It never entered my head about that sort of thing at the time. Well, I never let it.

I was just so focused on rugby league. I was so motivated, jumping hurdles all the time, it was case of 'bloody hell' this is fabulous.

Even when people put their feet out to trip us up, we simply lengthened our stride.

Nothing was going to put us off. We knew what we were about. We did not have the false belief that we were anything but lucky to be going to these places and playing. Most of our lads were rugby league. We didn't have any cross-coders, whereas the Army were 50/50.

They had experienced big tours and so on, but we didn't take it for granted. We never have in anything. Grounded seems a good word to describe the lads, then, now and always.

It's only when I look back that I have to take a deep breath and realise how much we had to contend with and how much the lads stuck at it.

I was always looking forward. While a lot of the guys

were thinking how great the tour was, I remember thinking we need to get official recognition and an annual dinner. The first of which we had in the Victory Services Club, London, attending the Challenge Cup Final in May 1996 beforehand, to celebrate achieving the milestone.

You can imagine how I felt after one particular watershed moment a year earlier, which came in the form of a letter to Air Chief Marshal Sir Michael Stear, head of RAF rugby union.

The letter was as a reaction after Air Vice-Marshal Feesey, our association president, had written to Bob Honey, (October 3, 1995) regarding the matter of Jeremy Handley announcing official recognition 18 months previously and the fact that we still hadn't got it.

To avoid making a decision for us alone, the plan saw Honey write what in many ways was a letter requesting approval to Stear, suggesting that rugby itself became a recognised sport, (both disciplines would come under the same umbrella) and that way we would both gain status.

On October 5, 1995, Honey wrote to Stear, to ask if they, union, would give the green light to this.

Can you imagine any other sport doing this, or being asked to come cap in hand, while the other code decides your fate? I can't envisage it ever happening.

I wasn't party to the response of Honey's letter, but it was always swings and roundabouts for us. I clearly remember only a few months before attending the House, we had gained official recognition. It was January 1 and Lorraine and I just went out for a meal, personally, no song and dance, no big article in *RAF News*, nobody seemed to want to make anything of it, except us. Association Wg Cdr Bruce Wynn and John Feesey, that was about it I suppose.

The landscape changed. We were due money from the

Sports Board, it was new territory, it was a case of 'bloody hell' we are official. We are entitled to this, that and so on.

I clearly remember the most significant thing I personally did to signal the change, that moment when nothing would ever be the same again. I sent out a letter to the lads for a fixture, putting a travel authority code on it.

I can still remember smiling to myself, as I sat in the Civil Aviation Authority in the Strand, London, writing the letters. I was so pleased for the team, who were just rugby league lads at heart. They had showed they wanted to play, had paid to travel all over the country to play for our sport, and so to suddenly be able to put that on the letter, to release them from their duties, it was brilliant.

We had really achieved something.

Here are some interesting financial facts to show you where rugby league is placed in comparison with other RAF sports associations. Figures provided by RAF Sports Lottery:

*Sports Lottery grants (non-public monies) 1994-2013:*
RAF rugby league: £120,000; RAF rugby union: £356,000 (inc Spitfires and Divisional teams); RAF football: £238,000 (inc referees tours and kit); RAF hockey: £147,000.

*Sports Lottery grants since start of 2005:*
RAF rugby league: £62,750; RAF rugby union: £150,980; RAF football: £132,000; RAF hockey: £65,340.

It was always like this though. It seemed we were pushing things along really well, then something would crop up or we would always have that 'big brother' thing looking over us with rugby union. But we were more cunning now, instead of just smashing through the walls that were put up, we dodged around them.

**Through Adversity**

When I look back, this period was a real learning experience and taught us, me especially, vital skills in this battle we were in.

If recognised status hadn't come, I would have knuckled down and got on with the job in hand anyway.

We would have always got what we were fighting for. I'm not being arrogant, we would never give up.

This is the best sport in the world and we know it. That keeps you fighting sometimes when all else seems lost.

For now, we had another victory under our belts and it was time to make great strides with it.

# Crapstone Villas

*26 April 1996*

*In rugby league history:* *6 April (1934): The French Rugby League was formed.*

*In RAF history:* *26 April (1944): VC: Sgt Norman Cyril Jackson, a flight engineer on No.106 Squadron, climbed onto the wing of his Lancaster in order to extinguish a fire during a bombing operation to Schweinfurt. He subsequently parachuted to the ground to become a PoW (London Gazette, 26 October 1945).*

LIFE in many ways is made up of singular moments, be they lines in the sand or a choice of which fork to take in the road.

I remember a calmness coming over me as I received the ball in the last few seconds of the Inter-Services match in June 1996, when a successful kick would draw us level, the best result we had produced so far in the IS. We, all those involved in RAF rugby league, knew what lay ahead.

I also knew, the second I collected the ball, that a

successful score would ensure the memory of coach Jack Wilson would remain, as it should do, in the hearts and minds of those involved in RAF rugby league.

In the main, I knew that I would make the kick, in part due to our first real coach's training and confidence-building skills. So as the ball sailed between the posts to ensure a 26-26 draw, we all somehow bid a fond farewell to the man known as Jack 'Effing' Wilson. Things would never be the same again.

It was not so much the house that Jack built, more a case of the footings that were put in place by his arrival and his no-messing attitude.

Turning up on the eve of the French Army game in October 1992, this brash, straight-talking Yorkshireman brought his combative approach to us at a time when we all really needed a bit of guidance. A pointer, maybe. Somebody to take the lead so that we could all find our feet that little bit quicker.

Wilson arrived in Uxbridge from Morley, where he would stay with Lorraine, Connor and myself on and off for the next three years. Having been sent to help us out by the RFL, he was a man steeped in rugby league expertise, an ex-pro, with some strange ideas. But for me he was manna from heaven. He was devoted to his backs, wanted to utilise them, and loved finesse.

He had this amazing ability to make you feel two inches taller. No matter what the situation or score, he would say his bit, put his glasses back on, spit a bit, swear a bit and then you were off, set for the battle.

More than that, his arrival was a sign that somebody cared about the obstacles we were climbing over, and us. He had pedigree, having coached at Dewsbury and Batley, and he had a colourful use of the Queen's English, which fitted in perfectly with the rest of us and helped bring us immediately together. He tried to look after us in his own special way sometimes; one of the stick-out ways of Jack was with Crapstone Villas.

The affectionately-named accommodation was given us by Jack's friend David Ward, Leeds and GB legend who since retiring from the game had earned his living through the Oakwell Motel, which he owned. He had always kept in touch with the game he loved, running an amateur league side out of the club and if we were ever in Batley playing, training and so on, we would go in with Jack to the club and stay there.

Wardy provided a warm welcome and most of all it was cheap. Every penny counted.

Following a few beers with a GB legend, Wardy would sometimes leave the lads to lock up after heading off half pissed into the night. We would all pile into the squash court area, which had the floor covered in mattresses, that was it, all of us stinking of beer, farting and snoring. Some of the lads bedded down in the sauna as well.

One morning we had two guys enter the sauna and then quickly leave when they saw the bodies strewn around the floor; on another one a guy started going through his weight lifting routine in the gym. As soon as he spotted all of us waking up, he quietly put the weights back down, picked up his towel and left. It was hilarious.

We also helped Wardy out on a couple of occasions, being called into the bar area if groups of lads were kicking off. Needless to say, when 'Spider' (aka James Le Mar), Al Blewitt and Co turned up, it didn't take long for the troublemakers to see sense and leave. Crapstone Villas may sound like a name for somewhere awful, but it wasn't. It was brill. We all hold it dear to our hearts.

## Through Adversity

On the night of Jack's death, we had done our usual preparations for the Army game, a side we had yet to beat, and were really up for getting that monkey off our backs. The Live TV satellite channel broadcast the match and we were to be shown after *Topless Darts*. This was the first real exposure we'd gained, among all that other sort of exposing during the 'arrers.

Jack had spoken to us all with his usual enthusiasm. He was meticulous and robust when he was talking tactics and gameplans; you never spoke when he was talking, and I mean never. He seemed on good form and left me to have a final word with the lads before leading them out. Funny now, but I recall seeing him go, never thinking for one second of the news we would hear when we returned for the half-time break.

It had been a combative affair, plenty of fights breaking out and we were losing heavily, so to hear the news that Jack had died of a heart attack before kick-off, well, we were devastated. Faces when the news was given stayed with me ... how people react and take news like that. It was an awful moment, but it was also the start of something new. Jack had helped us get this far and to give up now would have been wrong, pointless and also an insult to his memory.

I can imagine the language he would have fired at us if we had just gone into our shells, but we didn't. We all agreed to do it for Jack and the feeling just after my kick had cleared the posts was a strange mix of euphoria, tempered by sadness, then pride, as we all gathered together and hugged and chatted walking off the pitch. It is funny to think of one collective moment, unspoken, but acknowledged. We knew we had to crack on now. Jack wouldn't have had it any other way and neither would any of us in the same situation. His passing heralded a new dawn.

That in many ways was signalled when John Kear, RFL National Coaching Executive representative, gave a brief speech after the match. He mentioned among the obvious things, the standard that we had reached and how things were going in the right direction.

From this point, alongside chairman Wg Cdr Bruce Wynn, we had agreed on a strategic aim. We began discussing a tour to New Zealand. We opted for 'steady momentum' into 1997 and concentrated on the arrival of new Station teams such as the Uxbridge Blues, along with getting more people coaching badges.

It was a fabulous time and place to be if league was your game and it was awesome to have a southern Station dominated by rugby league.

The Blues team played in the London League and things were so full-on I didn't have to return home every weekend to play, it was all here on my doorstep. The RAF Regiment lads were there and we had people like 'Shifty' Healey, a Gunner, taking part in matches. These boys were tough and he still approaches me to talk about it to this day.

Another name is Andy Smales, a future RAF coach, who played at the Station.

The Inter-Service matches and the build up to them is completely different to anything else. To be fair, it is our total focus and initially, for me, it was about how we could show off rugby league. So I really concentrated on things like making sure the whitewash looked perfect and that the hospitality was right.

On the training field the work begins a few weeks before, and if the matches run consecutively we get that time together without a break, which is perfect.

Nowadays we get to use the A-grade players as well, which enables us to really work on opposition and defence stuff. We old hands who started it all back at Uxbridge only got together two days before a match, but not anymore. As an association we fully respect and work with the operational needs of our Service. This involves us moving people around so they are free for that point of the year, leaving us weaker in other places throughout the season.

We are willing to swallow this as it is our way. It is part of our core ethos that we are a Service first. It sees us jeopardise a lot of matches, such as the Challenge Cup, but it's all about September.

We do not use a 'Sports Marker'. That is a system that flags up a person as being involved in certain sports and who will be left out of certain tasks and so on, to ensure they are free for matches throughout their association's season.

Some have several players like this all year round. We don't. It is unfair on the Service to do that.

Our core beliefs are different. We are honest people who do not think we have a divine right to come and go as we please. We build that into our players. Our people get their teeth into Service life and their career in the same way they do their rugby league. Our ethos: no one player is bigger than the sport.

In the modern game we give our players a set of core values, if they do not buy into it then they will be RTU'd (Return To Unit) no matter who they are; we will not have it compromised. We also give them ownership of their own diet and training programmes. Admittedly, we help them out a lot. For example, in 2012 we utilised Middlesex University sports science undergraduates, who shadowed players, physically testing them throughout the Inter-Services to ensure they were at their peak to perform.

We are not all about power and muscle, like the Army for instance. We aim to produce flair and style on the pitch, but the players who are not fit enough will get found out. You need to be at your peak to play with flair and skill during a hard match or late in the game. In past years, we have competed physically with the Army for 60 minutes, now we want to do that for 80. The players see what efforts we are going to and they buy into that. We care about them and go that extra mile. We want them to raise their game.

The first time I saw the real value of this sort of thing was in 1999, when I was the fittest I have ever been and managed to run 40 metres to make a try-saving tackle after the ball had broke from a scrum and the opposition winger was running to the try line. To make that tackle was brilliant for me. I have never forgotten it. Being that fit and at your peak gives you an air of confidence. You have it about you and it becomes infectious.

Sport-wise I was buzzing. Things were going at 100mph. Our funding rose, my circle of friends quadrupled, players were coming out of the woodwork, league was everywhere around us.

Attending the Silk Cut Challenge Cup final pre-match dinner later that summer with Lorraine was an amazing moment ... pockets full of fags before the game as they were put on the table sitting alongside all the chairman of all the league clubs ... everyone chatting to us and inviting us to play at their grounds. I walked out rattling as I had pocketed so many cigs, being a smoker at the time.

Bob Connolly reffed the match, he of our 'broken arm clash', a few years previously.

The attitude of everyone towards us has never changed really. Today we have Steve MacNamara, England's head coach, welcoming us with open arms. As cheesy as it sounds, the rugby league family really exists.

Career-wise - yes there was one while all this was

going on - I was then posted to Bruggen in Germany. Bruggen was a flying unit and I had never been on one before, having spent all my time driving round London. There I was, watching Tornados take off as I approached the gate. The only time I had ever seen any of our planes previously was as gate guards, sat on a plinth!

Bruggen was a frontline Station and there I was, one of the youngest sergeants in the trade, thinking: 'How on earth do you refuel one of those?'

I had a steep learning curve and oversaw a team of guys whose job that was.

My main task there was to be responsible for Airfield Support, which meant controlling the refuelling tankers for the four squadrons of Tornados and also making sure that in inclement weather the runway was swept clean and always operational. The name for this is Op BLACKTOP.

My guys would also oversee plane push-backs, where the aircraft is literally pushed back onto the runway ready for take-off. It is all about fluid movement, making sure things run on time, all the time. I was very lucky to have some really good junior NCOs under me who knew their onions.

On a daily basis we would work with Eng Ops, establish flying programmes from each of the Squadrons. We could work out when they would be taking off and arriving from sorties. We would also have to factor in NATO aircraft that would be using the Station for refuelling, so it was a job with plenty of variety.

There really wasn't much difference in the job during the first Gulf War. Although the tempo of operations increased, as we were running smoothly, you really didn't notice much difference, although during Live Ops the aircraft would refuel on the way back as well.

It was just more focused, similar to a game scenario

really, once you cross the whitewash and all that. One aspect that really pleased me was seeing SACs really rise to their tasks. That is always pleasing and does not always happen.

Weeks before, my new boss Air Vice-Marshal Ron Elder, who funnily enough took over the presidency of the RAF RL, called me in to say I was being posted. He gave me time to think about it, but part of my decision was if I got to Germany could I still do my rugby league?

Bruggen (Bulldogs) had a great rugby league side, established for about four or five years, so straight away I was involved and of course that swayed my choice of posting.

Arriving as RAF team captain had its bonuses, but professionally I had a lot of people who wanted me to fall on my arse and sporting wise there were those wanting rugby league to do the same. But it didn't happen and it wasn't going to. The Station was massive. It had its own 18-hole golf course. It was a high-tempo place to work where everyone worked hard and played the same.

Arriving in August, we were setting off for New Zealand that October and our biggest tour to date, but in the intervening months I met up with a man who still to this day plays a massive part in the team and squad life: Corporal Dave Mortimer, the old sea dog or Shipmate as he is known.

It would soon become very apparent what an important part Shippers would play in the side. Everyone loved having him around, his attitude, stories and so on. His legacy began when he was offered the spot as kit man in the NZ tour. For the record he is the worst kit man in the world, but he is a legend. I met him training the Bulldogs. He was GDT Corporal (Ground Defence Training) and we hooked up on my first day at the Station, alongside Sgt Geordie Taylor, now the Armed Forces Development Officer.

When you arrive on a Station you have to go through

GDT, but to be honest the guys there knew who I was before I arrived.

There was a guy called Cpl Shaun Griffin, who played for the first team and was captain of the Bulldogs. I arrived, emptied my kit and went straight across for a cup of tea with Shaun, meeting up with Shippers.

After the initial welcome Dave showed me the ropes, and what ropes they were. During one beer-filled evening, it was discovered that we joined on the same day and that he was my deputy flight senior man throughout basic training.

So when I passed through No14 Flight RAF Swinderby he had overseen me. I remember this ex-marine and paratrooper, cycling naked through Swinderby when I was going through training and I was regaling him with this tale of this legendary guy and he piped up: 'That was me shipmate'. He told me the name of the other guy who was with him, Steve Harrison.

The penny dropped then, I can tell you. Although it must go on the record that cycling through Swinderby naked is a fairly relaxed day for Shippers, he has been round the block, you could say.

He was the driving force behind the ladies team and the kids (cubs) rugby league played at the Station, which Connor began to play in at the age of about three.

A lot of big names in the current Service game were based at Bruggen, our current association President Air Chief Marshal Sir Stuart Peach, then President of the Bulldogs side and a Wing Commander, Flt Lt Dean Andrew, OIC of the Bulldogs side and now Air Commodore and chairman of RAF RL among them.

I really had to hit the ground running at Bruggen. I had to take part in tanker pool training. I had to do the training there as a sergeant. I got amongst it, I need to do things properly personally, so I did jobs that the lads would do. I backed myself and it was all steady away to be honest. I could see all the guys who had been passed over for promotion moaning about me and what I was doing, but in other cases I had people who admired me for it.

I spent the first month there alone. Lorraine and Connor were back in the UK, and I remember going to dinner and sitting at the table with a WO. I was terrified. He asked me my age and what my trade was and when I told him '27' he nearly choked on his soup.

I also remember asking for a Becks in the mess bar that same night. The barman said: 'That'll be one D mate' (Deutsche mark) and I replied: 'No I'll have a big one,' meaning a pint. I was stunned when he said: 'That *is* for a big 'un mate.' Thirty-seven pence for a pint! Bloody hell.

Through the sport I fitted in quickly. I was meeting people who were now very good friends of mine.

Hitting the tarmac in Auckland, New Zealand, we had a new coach, David Busfield, and AVM Elder alongside us. We were greeted with the traditional touching noses Maori welcome.

This was no holiday. Busfield had us training straight off the aircraft. We played a base match first in the North Island, with 300 school kids doing the Haka for us before the match kicked off.

I remember the feeling of awe. What an experience for the young guys there, me included. Standing on the other side of the world, welcomed so well and to win all three games was just great. We were holed up in a hut, nails for hanging pegs and so on, but the main thing was we all stood together. We represented the Service, country and ourselves well. We took to it with glee; we appreciated where we were and what was going on around us.

Through Adversity

We had always had committed players and one example of that came when Butch Hainsworth began complaining about a toothache. He would have missed being involved if he had gone off to a dentist and was overheard asking where our physio Pete Morrison was, to see if he had some painkillers. Pistol Pete, as he as known, then offered to remove the tooth for the obviously distressed Hainsworth.

This was no ordinary tooth and we sat watching, partly laughing, partly in shock, as Hainsworth had this tusk removed; it must have been two feet long this thing.

Needless to say, after a big bit of tissue was jammed into the vacant space in Hainsworth's gum he was up and ready to get back to training. It was hilarious and also inspiring in a way.

Topping the whole thing off was a message back to the Chief of the Air Staff and all Station Commanders from AVM Elder, saying: 'RAF rugby league tour of New Zealand, played three, won three'. We gained great PR coverage afterwards. *RAF Active* ran a great article on us, which was superb when we returned home. That message was a fabulous endnote for us.

It was a time of great change, more was to come, but all the time I was learning to cope with things in a better way. I was growing and so was my beloved sport.

# In Sickness and in Health

*20 December 1999*

*In RAF history: 20 December (1956): Operation Musketeer; the last RAF personnel were withdrawn from Gamil Airfield after the RAF's short occupation of the Egyptian airfield.*

THE year had started really well. In March, we had held a meeting with the Navy about them playing in that year's Inter-Services for the first time. I went along with Coydy and we spoke with a guy called Wayne O'Kell, a Petty Officer who was their team coach. Wayne was from Leigh and knew his stuff. He was in many ways the Coyd and Clayton of Royal Navy rugby league.

We also met Chopper Smallbone, who was Navy and has one of the most memorable names I have ever heard, on a very memorable day for Services rugby league.

The meeting was held at the REME home at Arborfield, Reading, mainly because that's where Lt Col Mike Bowman was based.

## Through Adversity

He looked like George Dawes the bald baby comedy character from *Shooting Stars* and was the Army chairman, a lovely bloke, who held the meeting with the aforementioned.

We formally welcomed the Navy aboard. They were keen as mustard but for them it was easier, they were pushing at an open door. They knew the sport had been recognised and O'Kell wanted to get stuff squared away. For us, it added creditability to the tournament.

The pressure was then on though, nobody wanted the wooden spoon did they? Not now all three Services were involved. We were first up against the Navy at HMS Collingwood in Gosport that year. The match was not only one to remember, it set the seal as to the tempo of the clashes between the two Services from then on; never dull, always aggressive and always full of incident.

From our perspective we went into the game very confident after the draw with the Army. The bond we had garnered after that result and losing Jack was greater than we realised. RAF versus RN games are always played in a cauldron atmosphere, with plenty of stick coming from the crowd, so to lose a player early on just increased the atmosphere. The offence? The 'chinning' of O'Kell. Our player was innocent, though, and it still makes me laugh. We talk and goad each other about it to this day. O'Kell took a dive, the cheeky git. Our man, Gary Banford, was carded and we were a man down.

Banford had been playing at hooker. He passed the ball and O'Kell held his shirt back. He flung his arm back to shake the 'illegal' hand off, missing O'Kell, who then dived and all hell was let loose. Inadvertently that dive set the tone for all the matches played since.

We were right up against it after the break, despite leading at half-time. We were uphill against a vociferous crowd and the civilian referee and his touch judge, called Padre Wright, were about to play their trump card.

I remember defending two sets of six and then we cleared the ball. I was thinking we've done alright here, we are getting things back into order, then the Padre, who was terrible, almost as bad as the referee, gave them a scrum after giving an error against us. It wasn't and I called him, a man of the cloth this is, a 'cheating c**t'. We had been working so hard and we eventually got the ball and he cheats, a man of the church!

I couldn't believe it, so I called him what I did and he told the referee, who sent me off. That was the first time ever.

I was amazed I wasn't struck by lightning, but I was given plenty of abuse from the fans, as I had to walk right past the main stand to the changing rooms.

I was livid. I went into the changing rooms and I saw Banford's face It was a picture, one of absolute relief. You could see him thinking 'Oh thank God, it's not all my fault'. His face lit up. I'd been sent off, the bloody captain as well.

Banford needn't have worried. JT Ozzy Hicks at full-back led the team through, stepping up to kick a penalty and a drop-goal. He also made some crucial tackles, to see us through 27-24. It was a top display; he saved my blushes to say the least. Overall the Army had won the whole thing, spanking the Navy at Aldershot.

I returned to Bruggen with Station rugby being played across the board. These were the calmer times. The game seemed to mesh us all together, it was the blood going through the veins of daily lives. Then there was the first of the official British Forces Germany matches. I met Jason Talbot at a fixture against a British Students side.

The match was to launch the side but, for me, it ended up in a daze after I was knocked out in a tackle.

## Through Adversity

We got beat, I got hammered and all I remember about the first time I met Jason was that I don't remember anything about it.

He played and coached at Laarbruch and he came over to visit me to talk about rugby league. He is now the Combined Services secretary and also the performance analyst for the RAF 1ST XIII men's team. I know nothing about that meeting to this day.

Lorraine and I moved to Holland in 1999. I found out I was going to be posted, I had struggled with my age and rank in some people's eyes. I was up and running at Bruggen, 18 months in the post and I was competing well with my peers, who were much older than me. I had seen myself in this role and was not punching above my weight, more going along in the swim nicely, but my WO couldn't get his head round this 27-year-old Sgt Clayton doing so well.

I found that he and people would see me as somebody with time on my side. 'He's only a young lad, has plenty of time to progress', sort of thing. But I wanted to progress now. I found it frustrating. I was thinking I've performed well; I deserve my chance, no matter what my age. I knew I could either sit by and see what happened, or I could do something about it.

Deputy Commander in Chief Allied Forces North, Air Marshal Sir Christopher Coville, then came into the picture. I was approached to see if I wanted to work for him as his VIP driver and knowing what was going on around me, I thought it was time to get amongst it. So off I popped to a NATO base in Holland.

Rugby league was moving to summer and I was heading for a new challenge, long hours and a demanding job, but I wouldn't let it affect my game. I mentioned sport in my interview, he knew I was heavily involved, so I asked if I was going to be able to fulfil my commitment to rugby and there was no problem he could see.

I had an SAC working with me at that time and it was all going well. We moved across in August, I returned to England to play Inter-Services rugby league as the game had moved from May to September in line with the Super League, and then the world turned upside down.

I went to see a specialist at Heerlen Hospital in South Limburg, Holland, with Lorraine. He was a young guy who spoke good English, but in a very matter-of-fact tone. His first word as we sat there was: 'Look'. Every sentence started like that: 'Look'. I recall thinking: 'This is a bit harsh', but we, didn't know what to expect. You never expect cancer. Whatever it is you still don't expect that, until it's happened.

Cancer seemed to be the thing that happened to someone else, that's the sort of thing you feel. Selfish maybe, but it's the truth when you hear that word. The only reaction can be of utter disbelief.

It was September 22 when Lorraine fell ill. I was in England playing and she had spoken to Bruggen Medical Centre, who wanted to carry out a biopsy on some earlier test results. Lorraine was her usual buoyant self, saying on the phone: 'It will be alright, I'll be fine,' but I knew she was upset and so was I.

Looking back, there were moments that have shaped us as a couple today. There were experiences that have bonded us as lovers, as a family and brought out our true friends, people who came to the fore for us in a time of real need.

Lorraine went into hospital. I have no idea what the isolation must have been like for her at that moment; she knew nobody and had to call on friends who were in Germany. So she called Bruggen and they did a biopsy. I was called out of the bar after training and went to the

Guardroom and was told to go home. Lorraine was so strong, she was saying: 'Don't worry.' Despite her bravery I knew I had to get back to her. I shelved the game, the first Army match I had missed since 1994. Funny the things that stick in your mind while all else is in chaos.

From this point things go into something of a blur. I didn't know what was going on really. I hoped and thought it wasn't cancer, but in the back of Lorraine's mind I think she knew. Having been told 'look' several times by the specialist, we then heard the words, cervical cancer …

No more 'looks' then, just silence. Lorraine was catching her breath and I was devastated, complete shock, disbelief. It was just a case of 'shit, shit, shit.'

It is sadly true in life that at times like these people who are special really come into their own. It seems sad that it takes this sort of thing for people to really shine, but many did and I am still grateful to this day for that.

Work was superb. I had only just moved across to Holland and they just let me do what I needed. One guy, Flt Lt Billy Kidd, the boss's ADC, well nothing was too much for him. Time off was never a problem, whatever he could do.

Cpl Kev Barry was another and his wife, Judith, Matt and Tracey Knight and daughter Chloe, who Connor went to school with at the time, they became like surrogate parents to him. Looking back you really do find out who your friends are. Some people were embarrassed to talk about it, to broach the subject, some ignored me, some couldn't even manage eye contact.

It wasn't all doom and gloom. Inadvertently people made us laugh or gave us memories which still make us chuckle to this day. A fellow MT driver, Ian Aitkenhead, another great mate, gave us one of those memories at a barbecue just after Lorraine had been diagnosed.

We had a few people over at our house, Ian had his new girlfriend over and was talking as we were all standing around cooking and chatting. He starts talking, littered with swear words, saying: 'Yeah, cannot fucking believe it, my mate's dad, diagnosed with cancer, three weeks, dead.'

Well everyone just stopped and looked at him and he realised. It did us a favour, broke the ice. Lorraine preferred it that way, but it is very funny looking back now, as it was at the time. We fended things off that way, by laughing at them.

Another time at The Worsley Marriott Hotel in Manchester, just before the Grand Final in October, Ian was there, mucking about with Lorraine, of whom he was very fond, saying you are going to look like this and that, messing about, when Lorraine's parents came in. They hadn't seen their daughter since the diagnosis.

She got upset, so did Aitkenhead - well we all did - and the gravity hit us. Lorraine's treatment started and we found ourselves in a very lucky situation care-wise. We were next to a massive hospital that specialised in cancer and radiology.

Lorraine went in straight away for an operation. Doctor Stoot was the specialist and he operated to remove any infection. All the time Lorraine was positive about the whole thing. I was terrified, but dealing with things as best as I could. The operation was a major one, but I still didn't expect it to last 11 hours, three to four tops, but not 11.

I sat in the room with Lorraine's mum, Thelma, and we saw the doctor walk past. He looked finished, dreadful and my heart sank. I thought he was upset, not exhausted, and he began speaking, but didn't tell us if she was alright.

I thought she was dead. Thelma was in pieces and I was trying to work out, through this exhausted doctor's broken English, if my wife was dead or not.

## Through Adversity

I just blurted out: 'Fuck it, is she alright?' and he sort of stopped and repeated: 'Yes, yes, she is OK.'

Christ, the relief when he said it, and then he started explaining why things had taken so long. The cancer was Cat 2B and had been bigger than they thought.

We went to see her even though she was just out of theatre. I wanted to see her but, by the end of the visit, she probably wanted to slap me around the head.

Sitting in the room, Lorraine's mouth was really dry and they have a sort of sponge lollipop, which is damp, that's used to moisten the mouth. So I kept putting it to her mouth and just keeping it above her lips so she couldn't get it. Her lips were pursing, but she couldn't get to it. I was shot a look and knew the game was up.

From here on she had to undergo radiation treatment and our lives were submerged in the illness and the treatment of it. Lorraine never wavered one bit during the whole time, despite constantly feeling ill, having to stop doing things to be sick and so on, she never lost that fabulous sparkle.

We wanted to get away, and had already planned to do so with the Knights family to Bavaria as a way to celebrate the millennium and, of course, Lorraine didn't want to miss it. She was getting us all prepared for the trip, I was ready to cancel, but no she wasn't having any of it.

I can say without fear of contradiction that my wife is normally, but especially at this time, inspirational. We would go into the radiotherapy unit and she was 20 years younger than anyone else in there, but she just got on with it. Even when reality hits you in the face like that, to be able to do that is something special.

With a great sense of the ridiculous is how my wife deals with major things in life. During one treatment when they line you up to go in, she was sat in a wheelchair, drawings all over her body to tell the radiographer which area to treat, the gown that was being used to cover her had been taken off and she was naked.

The machine they were using suddenly broke and they had to move her, so up she went into a thing that looked like an office chair with wheels and they began wheeling her through the reception. She was saying: 'Morgen, morgen' to everyone, while trying to cover herself up. It was just another light at the end of the tunnel for us.

We convinced the doctors to give her a triple dose of radiation, so we could travel to Bavaria. Not an eyelid was batted by Lorraine, with sick bowl at the side of the bed and all that caper she kept on. We were going to have a great time with our friends, regardless.

The drugs had bunged her up during the trip. She hadn't been to the toilet and I clearly recall her saying one morning after another failed visit to the toilet: 'I am full of shit.' We all just cracked up.

It was things like that that lightened the whole thing up. And within what seemed like no time we were back to some form of normality.

Still some people could not talk about the subject, but we had lots of calls of support and well wishes. The strangest thing to me was how Lorraine just drew a line under it all. We had a nervous period during all the checks-ups. She had lost a lot of weight, but was insistent that I get back into organising the new season. She wanted me, and us, to get back in the groove. 'Don't worry about me.'

She was basically saying: 'you get back to playing rugby, because that's what we do.'

# Into the Navy

*7 September 2001*

*In RAF history: 7 September (1946): Gp Capt E.M. Donaldson, flying a Meteor F4 of the RAF High Speed Flight, established a world speed record of 615.81mph over a course off the Sussex coast.*

TO win the Inter-Services for the first time was a real milestone, everything we had been striving for in RAF rugby league. And, of course, the circumstances that led up to it on a personal level made it extra special; the Holy Grail. For Lorraine and me, it was the perfect ending and starting point.

We had been to hell and back, and then Halifax as it were, because we took the trophy to Main Street bar in that town after winning the final game and were made to feel like heroes by the rugby league-mad locals. It was really special.

Lorraine and I had already had a moment when the cup was brought in from the pitch after beating the Navy and I had caught her eye as we celebrated with Bruce Wynn and all the players' family and friends. I looked at her and things just fell into place. After all we had been through, personally and for the sport, we had done it and nobody could take that away from us. We had got the monkey off our backs. But we, as in Lorraine and I, had climbed a mountain together and the view was beautiful.

It had all looked a bit different in the run-up to the matches that year, because we had lost Jack Wilson in 1996 and been given a replacement in the shape of Dave Busfield, who was an ex-Halifax and Dewsbury coach and appointed by the RFL, in as much as they paid his expenses.

Buzzy and Jack were two different animals. Between them we learned loads, but they could not have been more apart in their approaches to the game and the men they were.

Buzzy was an ex-professional having played for Halifax and at Wembley for Featherstone. He was a big bloke who walked on his tiptoes. He had an air of confidence, even arrogance that came from his experience. He was a second row forward and he loved his forwards, especially when it came to coaching.

Jack had been a polar opposite. He was a back in his playing day and of course loved his backs. He was smaller than Bussy, with silver hair, wore glasses, and was also a bit arrogant in ways and could be very abrupt. But once you got inside that or got your head around it and won his friendship he couldn't do enough for you and showed what a really great guy he was.

Jack and I got on like a house on fire. Being a back myself, we thought the same way about the game, whereas Buzzy tore me off a strip once at half-time in one game over his bloody forwards.

There I was drinking my cuppa and he was talking to the team. I had my head down and he was quietly speaking, then he got next to me and roared: 'When my forwards are running, you pass them the fucking ball.' Well I spilt tea all over myself as I jumped in shock - third degree tea burns!

I took it mind and had a small bit of Clayton revenge during the second half when we had set up a forward line and I held onto the ball for a split second longer than usual and the forward took a massive hit.

The forwards suddenly didn't want the ball after that and we went on to win the game.

Another difference was in their approach to a match. Buzzy murdered us before kick-off. We were all knackered, he would put us through a full training session, whereas Jack just got us to do stretches and warm up together. They were different, but both brilliant for us and we learned a lot from them. Buzzy still comes to our annual dinner every year, he is a lovely bloke.

At the end of 2000 Busfield couldn't commit anymore, and we became the first service to employ a Serviceman as head coach. When we appointed Sgt Andy Smales, it was a statement and although our hand was sort of forced because Busfield had left due to other commitments, it was also in line with what we wanted, and that was to show that we, the RAF, were able to stand on our own two feet and fight our own corner, with our own people.

Within the first year we had achieved success, which was the main aim. Yes, we were playing in the Challenge Cup, but we had a good squad who just had not shaken the hoodoo of the Army, who had won the Inter-Services since 1998.

We never had problems against the Navy, although the games were always lively and intense, we just never shook off the Army. Everything we, I, had worked towards was the Inter-Services, so to win, and in some funny circumstances for the team, was incredible.

I learned a lot in that season, both personally and professionally. Some things in Damian Clayton were changed forever, some things that I wish had not been changed. But now looking back on it I realise they had to if I was to become the person I am today and to have been the person who dealt with the things that happened at that time.

We had been training at Linton-on-Ouse in the run-up to the matches and the build-up had gone anything but well. Always with Inter-Service matches there is massive apprehension and tension and unusually it boiled over and people started fighting during the training sessions.

The fighting started between Alex Killen and Butch Hainsworth after a terribly refereed session of 'touch and pass'. This became a truly significant part of the whole period of time, more so for me as I found out a lot about those around me. I trusted without thinking.

It was during the final sessions and the old sea dog Dave Mortimer was having a nightmare reffing it; he was not getting people back onside and people were getting annoyed and Hainsworth was one of those people.

You could never question Hainsworth's commitment. He might have homemade tattoos on his hands, but he was a stalwart player when it came to the cause of RAF rugby league. A 100 per cent man, what you saw was what you got with him.

He looks like he's been bobbing apples in chip fat he is that beaten up, and then there was Killen, a big lad from Widnes, another one who had been there from the start and played whatever. Both were proper rugby league men and this was their moment.

The fight was split up, Smales told them to shake on it and get refocused on the game the next day. They shook hands and within moments of the next play starting they were at it again, everyone began shouting and screaming. Killen lost it and told Smales he was off, to which Smales replied: 'If you go now, that's it, you won't be coming back.'

Sadly, and I say that to this day because his actions led to him missing out on something that he had worked and fought for all those years, Killen was gone. He got in his car and drove off. He would never come back and he would never see or share in the moment of winning that trophy.

It is one of my biggest disappointments that Alex Killen wasn't part of it. Don't get me wrong, he was abrasive and rubbed people up the wrong way, but when I look back now it was horrible for him.

A lot of things came out as a result of that incident, and a lot of people failed to put their hands up and say what had actually happened. People who I had thought were solid, trustworthy people allowed me to shoulder the blame for a lot of it, rather than setting the record straight.

The day of the first match against the Army, Smales rang RAF Wittering and spoke to Killen's boss, it was more a duty of care thing, to check personnel were safe. So he rang this fellow and checked that Killen had returned back safely, saying he was no longer with us.

His boss didn't know who it was that had called and Killen assumed, wrongly, it was me who made the phone call, since when he has a personal vendetta against me.

He thought I was checking up on him, but people who knew it wasn't me didn't speak up, preferring to let me take the rap.

Rather than speak up, they allowed a situation where Alex venomously hates me to build and now it has built to the extent where he has ignored me in pubs, been playing and hurled abuse at me, worn T-shirts under his shirt at the Inter-Stations final for Odiham, where I was on RAF rugby league secretary duty, sporting the words: 'If you aren't part of Clayton's train set, you won't play'.

Another time when I was a Sergeant at Leeming and took a phone call from Ali-Al-Salem airbase in Kuwait, it was a bad line, but it was Killen on the other end hurling abuse at me. This thing has been allowed to snowball when it could have been nipped in the bud, but now it has become too long in the tooth and I think it is sad.

I was good mates with Killen, we had been through thick and thin. So to see it had eaten away at him and nobody had done anything about it, when they could have was a big frustration. Not one of them had the balls to tell the truth.

I have never changed the way I do business, but I learned that the people I assumed had the moral courage, didn't.

I speak my mind and let people know what I think. This may have mellowed as I have got older, but I learned from that point that I need to be careful when assuming things. It is alright when things are going well, but there will always be a slump and I never looked at that. Some people prepare for that and make sure they are not going to be affected by it. I don't. Maybe it was because I may have been getting a bit of success they thought; he can have some shit as well.

I now know people don't have the same moral fortitude that I have. I have not become apprehensive, but I do look before I jump. I now make sure people have ownership of things, that my head isn't always on the block, so I am not the one left holding the baby. It saddens me that I have had to change like that.

The fight had not changed anything in many ways. Killen was a good player, but a lot of the players didn't like him, he was disruptive. So we may have lost a good player, but in the eyes of the new players they had only lost a bad influence.

On the morning of the game we were ready. We were playing at York City Knights RL home ground Huntingdon Stadium, the weather was bad, and we started the game with two badly broken leg injuries in the opening 15 minutes.

Cpl Andrew Gillett, 'Gilly', who played at centre, went down early doors after a nothing challenge and then the Army scored.

A second player, Cpl Scott Simon, who played for London Broncos and was prop for us, a great prospect, then went down with a spiral break. That's a really bad break, all the way down the centre of the leg.

As captain I tried to rally the troops, but what that side achieved was incredible. It was for me the first time I really identified the 'mateship' that has become so integral to us as a team, an association and me as a person on the pitch. We murdered them, not just with good rugby, but all across the pitch. Everybody rose to the challenge.

One of the things that will live with me was the changing room at half-time. We were leading, but only just. I looked around that room and I thought; 'We are going to win this'. It's difficult to describe, but I just knew.

A friendship was also built on that day when I was awarded the man of the match by the Director of the RAF Sports Board, Air Vice-Marshal Chris Davison.

It was his first introduction to Royal Air Force rugby league and to beat an Army team 34-14 was great for him as well as us. We enjoyed the night and then it was all to play for at Wakefield against the Navy; we needed to win and the trophy was ours, simple as that.

It was really funny before that game, because Jerry Rushworth was playing for us then and we were in the tunnel waiting to be led out before the match and Connor was the mascot, aged about seven.

So the Navy captain is there, Izzy Gay, and he is obviously thinking: 'If I get at Clayton I can stop them playing as he is the playmaker and captain.' Poor Connor's face, there is a picture of it in this book, he looks terrified, bless him, sheepish to say the least.

Rushworth almost started hitting Gay, throwing abuse back at him: 'You fucking leave him alone you fucking wanker or I'll give you some to shout about,' he was roaring, so it was all happening and a great atmosphere.

This was another match we dominated. But of course you had to go through the mill to get there, never easy with the RAF and the referees we used to get.

Right at the death SAC Scott Andrew scored a length of the pitch try and we were celebrating, but the touch judge 90 metres back had pulled us for a forward pass, so there we were, forced to dig in. I thought it won't happen, but finally the whistle was blown. We started celebrating, but it wasn't a whistle for the end, it was for a penalty, and the referee then played about 10 minutes of injury-time, which we somehow managed to hold on for and take the win.

I suppose people could say it was like playing Man United, with the amount of time he gave at the end. When the whistle did go, the relief of the moment was draining.

To see our Chairman, Air Commodore Bruce Wynn's face and give him a hug when we had won, that will live with me. We were up and running.

I was delighted for a lot of people, such as Smales, it was brilliant. We as a Service had stood alone and we had benefitted from it. We were the first to win like that, it was a massive step forward. We could now be held up as an example of how Services could represent themselves.

## Through Adversity

Most of the success had come because Smales, being a Serviceman, had helped us build the first real foundations for ourselves.

I learned just how important my sport could be within months of that victory when I was posted to the Falklands the next year, in February 2002, as SNCO IC Tanker Pool aircraft refuelling flight, which meant overseeing the refuelling of the resident Tornados, Hercules, Tristars and visiting aircraft. There I was on an island that had 100mph crosswinds, everything covered in goose shit from the Upland geese, with nothing else to do than either drink or go down the gym. So I organised a rugby league match.

There must have been 1,500 troops there back then and we played the Resident Infantry Company. After all we had been through I recall thinking to myself, here I am, nearly 8,000 miles away from home and they still cannot stop us from playing.

We can play and we will play, so up your arse.

# Most Excellent

*14 June 2002*

*In rugby league history:* 14 June (1924): St George defeated reigning premiers Easts 9-0 at the Sports Ground in front of 1,500 spectators. St George finished fifth overall that season.

*In RAF history:* 14 June (1991): Flt Lt Julie Gibson became the first female regular RAF officer to be awarded her pilot wings when she graduated at No. 6 FTS, RAF Finningley.

I WAS 8,000 miles from home as 2001 was drawing to a close and things were about to change at the top of RAF rugby league, but when were we not used to that?

Even though it would be another case of through adversity, this time our future would be decided and secured in many ways through the ill hand of fate. In my absence there had been a lot of tinkering and note making, all of an amazing kind that would change my life forever and give me a real belief that all the efforts I had put in were worthwhile and being recognised.

## Through Adversity

While I was getting friendly with the penguins, the Association's now President, Gp Capt Bruce Wynn, had been in cahoots with new chairman Wg Cdr Nick Mawston preparing a citation for a state honour. Wynn had been involved from the very start, way back in 1994, and having seen us win the Inter-Services for the first time and following his promotion to Air Commodore, he, of course, took up the role of Presidency, bringing in Wing Commander Mawston as Chairman in the middle of that same year.

Now, to be fair, from the start Nick was much more into the business side of things, he was not a league man.

He was from the Midlands and working with him taught me a lot of diplomacy skills. Not in a bad way, he was a lovely bloke, just we had not been used to working with somebody other than Wynn, with whom in many ways myself and team coach Smalesy would say we want this and he would organise it for us or lean on the appropriate people.

I know that Nick was involved in writing up the citation and I still believe to this day that the reason behind it was the IS win.

I had arrived back from the Falklands in April 2002 and was working in MT Trade Training and Licensing at RAF Leeming. Trade Training and Licensing entails ensuring all personnel are confident using and familiarised with driving whatever vehicle we have available in the Service.

It is a Tri-Service responsibility, and comes as part of the FMT 600 MoD driving licence, so if somebody needs to use a Land Rover, we train them in using it. It can involve anything really. If they are using a lorry we would train them on the road, if a Land Rover, then off-road.

It was in June and I was having a really shit day. I called Lorraine to try to cheer me up, she usually manages it and on this day she couldn't have done it any better.

I called and asked for some good news. The phone went really quiet, and she said; 'You won't believe it, I've got a letter here, it looked official so I opened it.'

Well, my heart started going. I asked her what it was and reading from the letter she said: 'Her Majesty The Queen has awarded you the Most Excellent Order of the British Empire'.

'FUCKING HELL.'

I nearly dropped on the floor, but there was a caveat with the letter that stated I wasn't allowed to tell anyone.

Well, of course, Lorraine had opened the letter, so she knew, and I couldn't contain news like that. I was on top of the world so I went straight to my MTO (Mechanical Transport Officer), WO Paddy Kelly, and told him. What an incredible feeling that was. I liked the way he worked and grinning from ear-to-ear off I went. We were expected to go down to the Palace in the November, but my more immediate feeling was that Lorraine and myself had gained formal recognition for all the hard graft. It was another part of my constant self-actualisation process. I saw myself pushing on. I did see it as recognition for my sport, but also for my efforts.

Some people muttered their disapproval, but I was getting used to that!

The number of letters I got within Armed Forces RL was amazing. For example, Lt Col Jeremy Bethell and Lt Cdr Nick Stenhouse, from Army and Royal Navy RL respectively, were very proud I and the game had got the recognition it deserves.

Lt Col JJ Bethell wrote: 'Your award is thoroughly deserved. You have contributed so much to Service rugby league, playing the most tremendous role in helping so many airmen, as well as the soldiers and sailors they have played both with and against, experience this fantastic game.'

Stenhouse wrote: 'From us all at RNRL, very well done on the award of your MBE, we are all delighted for you and your family. I know only too well how much time and effort is required in keeping a representative sport on the road.'

The one abiding moment was with Lorraine though. We had been through the ringer and her telling me down the phone will always live with me; it was a wonderful moment to share with her.

They could take away all of the memories attached to that passage of my life, except that one, it was special. I'd fight them to keep that one.

I was also a bit embarrassed because Martin Coyd had not received anything and we had sort of built up Service RL between us. Even so, he was on the phone congratulating me, as I was when he was entered into the rugby league Roll of Honour recently. It was just rewards for a great and hard-working bloke and a proper rugby league man.

So in the November we went down to Buckingham Palace. I met a few civvy friends who I had driven mad with rugby league in those early days while I worked at CAA (Civil Aviation Authority) House. Pete Celeschi, Heather Blowers, Lorraine, myself, our Connor, who was only about eight years old, and my mum spent a few days in London, had a few bottles of champagne and saw the sights. We did it right.

I was gob-smacked on the day, really. I had never been nominated for anything before and then 'bang' there was this. I had a State Award.

On the big day it was the pageantry that got me, we do that better than anyone else don't we? I remember being led in and lined up to one side with these large screens showing previous ceremonies. I didn't realise until the day that I was the first Serviceman to be awarded for 'sole contribution to sport', which made me very proud.

I also helped ease England rugby union star Jason Leonard's nerves on the day. There was this England star, who I think went on to be nominated for an OBE, standing on his own in his morning suit. I saw him and went over and started chatting about a few things and he told me who he was. I knew already and my first words to him jokingly were: 'What have you got your award for?', which broke the ice.

He was playing at Harlequins at the time and Gary Connolly, a rugby league lad, had gone there from St Helens, so we spoke about that. We had a right laugh in general and he went from being totally out of his comfort zone to cracking up laughing with me. Afterwards he brought his family over and asked to pose in some shots with us. I thought that was a nice touch, the two codes together.

Another nice touch was seeing Wing Commander Mawston standing outside the gates as we drove out. We stopped and he congratulated me. It was a terrific thing to do and the mark of the type of man he was. An abiding memory was the media coverage it gained for the association and Services rugby league. John Knighton from BFBS had been to visit me to carry out an interview for the channel and they obtained a copy of me receiving my MBE from Her Majesty and ran it moments afterwards on the channel.

I found myself moving from Leeming in January 2004, on promotion as a Flight Sergeant, to go to Halton and what a world of difference my new posting was to be, talk about understanding self-actualisation.

I had never instructed before and I was to be part of a team of trainers instructing the future senior NCOs of the RAF as part of the IMLC (Intermediate Management and Leadership Course) at ACS (Airmen Command Squadron).

## Through Adversity

We had a three-week set-up as part of the Supernumerary DS, so there was a lot of preparation, which was key to producing the goods during the training. I never went into a lesson without knowing all I needed to know and then some. I had standards and the guys and girls I was instructing would realise that and learn from it, hopefully wanting to have the same standards. I would advise anyone to do that course. It is brilliant. I cannot speak highly enough of it. You learn so much about your Service and yourself.

There was one incident that really showed this, when an outside company that was being used to instruct on Air Power could not deliver the course required and myself, Steve Cartwright (now WO) and FS Keith Flannigan just said 'yes' we would do it, we would learn this course in quick time and teach it. Others looked at their shoes, but we stood out and said 'yes'.

I never wanted to compromise myself and studied as much as possible. We were introducing new things to the Service, right at the cutting edge, it was brilliant.

There is one thing called the OODA loop (Observe, Orientate, Decide, Act) and I was instructing it. I got two NCOs to put blindfolds on in the lecture hall at Halton. One guy was prepped beforehand, knowing he had to tackle the other fella when I said a key word. They were moving around the stage and I was talking about what their decision should be. I told them to find each other and the prepped guy fell to his knees as instructed and rugby tackled the other, causing him to fall headfirst into the lectern.

He hit his head and it could have been a nightmare, everyone was laughing, but I was thinking: 'Oh, bloody hell!' The bloke was fine, though, and took it in good heart.

In another lecture I was bouncing around the stage, you could say I am enthusiastic when I give my lectures. So there I was jumping around and I fell off the bloody platform. I had to send the whole lot of them for a cuppa and a half-hour break as they were laughing so much. Pillock.

On the field things came down to earth with a bump, as we were to find out that defending a title is completely different to winning one. We were battered by the Army and ended up with the wooden spoon.

The match at Dewsbury was lost in the first 20 minutes. We were just caught cold and I remember Smales coming into the changing room to give us a rocket. He went to kick all the water bottles situated in the middle of the floor to make an impact, but he stopped halfway through and ended up tapping them. Never one to hold my tongue I told him afterwards that if he was going to kick them then do it properly, like Alex Ferguson. It wasn't much fun out on the pitch though.

Nor was the phone call that said Wg Cdr Mawston had died. It was a devastating shock, an awful moment; he was on his way to work, aged just 43. As I said, Wynn had sort of forced Nick upon our association initially; he was a hands-on type of person and we just were not used to that.

I remember him asking me about the points for a field-goal and so on, but due to the hierarchy of the Service, we had to be diplomatic in persuading him to see things our way. I was still a Sergeant at this time and had no real right to be dealing with him or telling him what to do, so we had to tread very carefully at first.

Being the type of person he was, Nick went on to become a real part of the set-up. He used to bring his son down to matches and we built up a great rapport with him and paid our respects to a good man at the RAF St Clement Danes Church in London. I attended with women's rugby league team captain Sgt Vicky Dillon.

It was from this moment of tragedy, though, that our future began to form. We could not be a rudderless ship, so quickly after losing Nick I approached Deano, whom I had first met in Germany as a Flight Lieutenant.

He was the Chairman of British Forces Germany RL and, oddly enough, we had first been in contact through another moment of tragedy, when he wrote to me to tell me JT Archie Monks, who had toured in Morocco with us on the Joint Services tour in 1994, had died.

To get Deano as our Chairman was a great boost. It was a no-brainer for him, a dyed in the wool Hull man, black and white through and through.

He would cycle to work, when he was stationed at Marham with 31 Sqn, whistling 'Old Faithful', the Hull RLFC song, while taking a salute off personnel at the main gate as he rode by. Fantastic.

Let's put it this way, Wing Commanders don't come out of Hull and he had done very well for himself, so to have him involved was excellent. He was one of us and it was the start of the present really.

What followed may not have been one of the most exciting periods of RAF RL history, but we were doing alright and it saw me as a person developing and the association trying new things, for example, the Coningsby 9s Stations event. We also built up a good rapport with Sky Sports, especially their presenter Angela Powers, and were regularly featured on *Boots 'N All*.

Although the relationship started slowly on a personal level, Deano then facilitated Air Vice-Marshal Peach to become our President after Wynn had stepped down, retiring from the RAF. It was another major move forward.

Wynn was honest enough. He said he couldn't give us the attention and commitment we deserved, which I really respected him for, especially as he had been with us all the way. He and his wife Sian are still and will always be a massive part of the RAF RL family. They still come along to the end of season dinner and it is always great to see and catch up with them.

Air Vice-Marshal Peach came in and was initially fairly distant. He had been involved with rugby league before while stationed at RAF Bruggen and, I think from what I know of him now, he likes the adversity that we seem to face as a sport and association. His posture was completely the opposite to Deano, who in his Flt Lt days was like Tigger on Speed, he is such an effervescent bloke.

We were now dealing with all sorts of people and one of the biggest things to ever happen for our association came immediately after their appointments, a vital part of our make-up today, the sponsorship through BAE Systems.

This was started purely due to Peach being in post. Mo Stevens and Kevin Porter of that company have become our life-blood and they have stuck with us; their support to this day is brilliant. We have a fantastic partnership with them.

There is no need to be naive as to how the world works; they wanted access to Peach and he knew we needed their support. To have a major corporate sponsor was incredible and he secured this.

I met Mo and director of Business Development Kevin for the first time at RAF Uxbridge, when they and I were posing for a squad photograph before we went off to New Zealand on our 2005 tour.

I can honestly say that we could not have achieved as much, or continue to do so, without the help of outside sponsors. They feel part of the team and get a lot out of their involvement and it's important to us that they do. We have other sponsors on a smaller scale, all vitally important people, such as Mark Gear and Graham Bradley, who are local builder pals of mine. They help us out with sponsorship, throwing in a 'bag of sand' whenever we need it!

But whatever the level of help, each person and company has become part of the RAF rugby league family.

*Above*: Damian Clayton MBE, pictured with the RL England Training Squad
*Below*: In the thick of the action, as usual, against the Royal Navy

*Right*: Post sortie
with GB captain
Paul Sculthorpe

*Left*: Old Trafford
Super League
trophy guard with
Wayne O'Kell MBE

*Above*: My first Sky Sports interview, after a Joint Service v French Army fixture

*Below*: Enjoying an Inter Station Cup final win with RAF Coningsby in 2012

*Above*: With Jack Wilson, prior to meeting the King of Morrocco

*Below*: Lance Bombardier Ben Parkinson meets England's Rob Purdham at Doncaster

*Above*: The RAF first team squad with
Bruce Wynn and coach Dave Busfield,
pictured in 1999

*Right*: The legend that is Dave
Mortimer - irreplaceable

*Left*: Kicking duties
for the Combined
Services

*Below*: Fulfilling
Community Board
duties prior to the
2011 Super League
Grand Final at
Old Trafford

*Top*: Sir Stuart Peach, preparing to present the Challenge Cup at Wembley
*Middle*: History in the making - The Blue Bombers prepare to fly in 1992
*Bottom*: The early days with Uxbridge Blues, after winning the London
League Shield at Chiswick

*Above*: The mighty Bruggen Bulldogs prior to an Inter Station Cup final - we lost!

*Right*: Chris Gordon scores a Great Britain try in the 2013 Armed Forces World Cup

*Below right*: Connor receiving his RL Cub award from Dave Morts at RAF Bruggen

*Below*: Representing Combined Services against BARLA in Scotland

# WAR BLIMEY

## Afghan crisis can't ground RAF Cup bid

*Above*: Coaching rugby league to the kids with Deano in Kingston, Jamaica

### By Geoff SWEET EXCLUSIVE

HE Royal Air Force will today put the horrors of the Afghan to one side as they to keep their llenge Cup bid flying

a team, formed, just years ago, is just one away from a possible ting with a Super ue side – not bad for a whose players train to- r only ree of ason an

in Oman. Sgt Clayton, a transport manager, based at RAF Leeming in Yorkshire, said: "The team is scattered all over the country but poor Andy is worst-hit.

"He's on active service in the supporting the anti-terror-

Twin Towers tragedy. Like all of us, he knows how big this game is because a victory – and we're confident we can hold Leigh – would win us the experience of a lifetime in facing a Super League club.

"Mind you, I won't be there if we go through – I'm off to the Falklands on December 28!

"I'll be heartbroken because I formed the team back in 1993 and I've been dreaming about playing Wigan or one of the big boys ever since.

"We are lightweight because

in Middlesex, is up with problems drawn from bas country and the all train in the the same time.

But the demar ghan conflict has normal pressure

Clayton said: unsettled team. the front line a but we have to c personnel who e "So it's diffic getting together Prop Terry hooker Butch ten trying hard match atmo a meeting

*Above*: Enjoying a laugh with Deano before the CS v GB Police clash

*Left*: Wayne Bennett imparts his knowledge to SAC Johnny Ledger

*Below*: FS Dave Mortimer Armed Forces RL farewell top table in August 2012

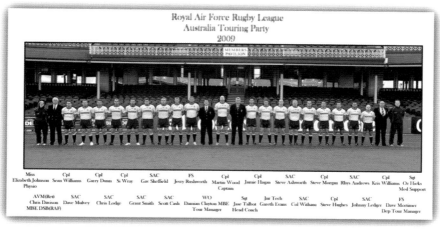

Royal Air Force Rugby League
Australia Touring Party
2009

Miss Elizabeth Johnson Physio | Cpl Sean Williams | Cpl Garry Dunn | Cpl Si Wray | SAC Gav Sheffield | FS Jerry Rushworth | Cpl Martin Wood Captain | Cpl Jamie Hagan | SAC Steve Ashworth | Cpl Steve Morgan | SAC Rhys Andrews | Cpl Kris Williams | Sgt Oz Hicks Med Support

AVM(Ret) Chris Davison MBE DSB(RAF) | SAC Dave Mulvey | SAC Chris Lodge | SAC Grant Smith | SAC Scott Cauls | WO Damian Clayton MBE Tour Manager | Sgt Jase Talbot Head Coach | Jnr Tech Gareth Evans | SAC Col Witham | Cpl Steve Hughes | SAC Johnny Lediger | FS Dave Mortimer Dep Tour Manager

*Above*: The RAF RL Australia touring party and our historic photo taken at the Sydney Cricket Ground

*Right:* Presentations after a clean sweep, with AVM Ron Elder and Gp Capt Bruce Wynn enjoying the moment

*Above:* Meeting Prime Minister Tony Blair, while on Operations

*Right*: Playing rugby league in the Falkland Islands

*Above*: Champagne with Heather and Peter prior to receiving the MBE and, *inset*, Ian - a true friend (albeit one whose foot is usually in his mouth!)

*Right*: It's finally ours! Here I'm being presented with the Inter Service trophy in 2001

*Below right*: RAF v Royal Navy - an over-awed Connor senses the pre-match tension

*Below*: Lorraine, Connor, Mum, me at Buckingham Palace and, *inset*, Lorraine and Connor after a Halifax U20 match

# Go East, Young Men

*12 April 1996*

*In RAF history:* 12 April (1940): Heavy daylight losses finally convinced Bomber Command that self-defending daylight bomber formation theory was not valid, marking the most important turning point in Bomber Command's war.

*In rugby league history:* 12 April (1909): Warrington inflicted upon St Helens their record defeat, 78-6.

IN many sporting situations there is an unwritten rule: what goes on tour, stays on tour. But in our case 2005/06 produced two tours that saw us bring what went on tour home.

The trips, especially the 2006 voyage to Moscow, were ground-breaking, not only personally, but also for the Service and the great sport of rugby league.

The year 2005 had seen us return, amidst a flurry of activity on the home front, to New Zealand. Our first visit had been in 1997, which was then followed by a return tour, where we hosted the NZ side the next year, when the visitors won. The matches saw us play a re-enactment of the historic All Gold versus Northern Union games. The home match was played at the Halliwell Jones Stadium, Warrington, with a further game played there in 2007, entitled the 'Centenary International'.

This latest tour had been organised by Jason Talbot, in fact it was the most proactive I have ever seen him. He was inspired, or just fed up with the lads who had gone on the 1997 trip going on about how great it had been. He was on a hiding to nothing, as you can never repeat such an amazing tour, which saw us win everything, but to be fair he did a bloody good job, and although we did not have as strong a side as in 1997 we had a great time with Butch Hainsworth bowing out from the team. The youngsters with us developed and learned because of it, with some excellent opportunities to interact with the NZ Warriors side, who we watched train.

For me, at 36, it was a great opportunity to rub shoulders with the NZ CAF AVM Graham Lintott and his WO, Keith Gill. There I was talking about strategies within the Service and the sport alongside Deano, while the younger lads got pissed. It was strange but it was also the right way to be going and once again I thrived on it.

I can fully recall doing the business, not just as the captain on the pitch, but also as a cog of growing importance off it. If we as a sport and Service were to continue playing then we and by we, I mean myself, would have to stretch ourselves to keep the RAF brand out there. We have been back in touch with Lintott as part of the 2013 Defence Rugby League World Cup, with Deano contacting him recently, so the relationship we built up is now a strong one and is seeing the sport expand and include more countries and Services.

Organising trips abroad can be really tiresome if truth

be known. There is so much that goes into it and so much to do when you are away that it can detract from your own tour. In Australia, in 2009, I wanted the lads to experience State of Origin. That was the main reason for going there.

I started planning for that two years before departure. Getting the RFL to check the recipients who wanted us there was the first port of call, then I had a check list to complete for both the Sports Board - to enable us to get lottery funding which, to be honest, none of these trips would happen without - and the RFL. I had a flow chart set up to ensure that all the right protocols were adhered to. We then had to get diplomatic clearance, get the governing bodies to sanction the tour and set about getting the guys freed up, which is never easy. There's also sorting out the money and payments for numerous other things.

Looking at the playing personnel, which is pretty important, I have never gone on tour with the best team we have available at the time because of the demands of Service life and duties, which we are always mindful of and fit in with. You also have to decide upon who is in charge while abroad and then nanny some of the guys when they are there, in case they get a bit carried away. In Australia, I had one guy missing ten minutes before the bus was to leave for the airport. It was a panicky moment, but he had just been out enjoying himself and we all made it onto the flight.

The Moscow trip in 2006 was something very special and strange, in a way that only Russia can be.

Deano had been offered the tour by the RFL as part of its expansion programme. The Army had turned the trip down, but it did seem more appropriate for the RAF to go, having had such a close involvement during the Cold War as the first line of defence and so on. Well I thought so anyway. Deano jumped at the chance and the goodwill, superb PR and in fact international political relations that came about as a result of just one match was incredible. We ended up playing in a place called Krasnokamensk, also known as the Forbidden City, which was built to commemorate Yuri Gagarin's first ever-manned space flight. The last Westerner to see this was Jacques Chirac, former French president, and the air attaché told us that as a result of our tour he had carried out more business than in the previous five years.

In truth there is not much to see in the Forbidden City, it is made up of very drab buildings, has a large checkpoint at the front, a large statue of Lenin and a large town hall, which is very grand inside. It is the opposite of Red Square, which is truly spectacular, colourful and, well, inspiring.

Krasnokamensk is eerie, unnerving and had that effect on the lads as well. When they arrived the banter on the coach fell silent as soon as we reached the checkpoint, I can tell you. The only comparison I can give anyone who has spent time on a military station is that it is far drabber than anything we have in the UK. Like the Russian people, who rarely smile and seem very hard on the exterior, it, and they, were very welcoming once you get to know them a little.

Flt Lt Mark Fothergill and myself undertook the initial reconnaissance trip to Russia, Fothers was from Halton and had organised the trip, but I found it funny how I was the one who took the lead once we'd arrived and would help guide him throughout the initial phases and then on the tour itself. Things were changing for young Master Clayton.

So there we were at Moscow Airport in March 2006 and we were taken to the British Embassy. We were told en route to expect our rooms to be 'done over' even if it was only as a warning. *Tinker Tailor Soldier Spy* come to life I thought, except on their side of the fence, not ours. I got my room and squared away my admin and had a shower, wanting to go out for a few light ales. I remember thinking as I dried myself off, 'Are they filming me?' So I quickly covered up, not wanting to make anyone laugh at my manhood.

I collected Fothers, whose room was like a grenade range, and we went with Sgt Nicky Gould to the Hard Rock Café and had a meal. I returned to my room and, of course, things had gone to type, everything was turned over. I have no idea what they thought they were going to find, but when I went down to Fothers' tip, they had tidied it up for him.

What an insult I thought, but we knew they had been there, so their job was done. When we arrived with the team we had a tail on us everywhere we went. It was surreal and bizarre. We used to try and spot them, but even if we couldn't we knew they were there.

The Russian Air Force is known as Space Forces and we were taken to meet up with their attaché or head for this tour at the Russian version of the MoD building, opposite the Kremlin. What a setting and funny encounter. I found myself driving there and we met a a blond-haired PTI called Colonel Victor Pototski, who was heading the tour up.

He was a rough-looking sod, but had kind eyes and I built up a bit of a bond with him. I warmed to him you might say. His voice was aggressive, but we organised a few things, with his bloody mobile going off throughout the meeting.

I held my tongue and I learned further things about diplomacy through that one simple act.

Once we had finished we went to look at the pitch. It was one of the third-generation pitches, so no studs would take. I walked around and looked at it, piles of snow around the edges and so on, it was freezing. Then as we began to speak with Pototski about the match, agreeing that it was fine, he apologised about his phone ringing and told us it was his birthday and that his family and friends were ringing about a big party to be held that night. I smiled and tried to imagine him tucking into jelly and ice cream, but was truly taken aback when he invited us to attend.

We went to the party and we were treated as minor celebrities, before they began talking about going for a swim at this big centre. I ducked out, but Fothers went for it, stripping off he was doing backstroke in front of all these Russian Military people. I thought it was hilarious. He could have at least stayed on his front instead of using his old boy as some sort of mast. During the tour the following month, we were followed everywhere. We had one game to play, which was an 11am kick-off, and were chaperoned by a guy who became known as Bullet Tooth Tony, after his gold teeth. It was a perfect name.

So picture the scene, 5000 Russian conscripts marching up and down putting on a show of strength and the AVM of the RAF Sports Board, Chris Davison, and Fothers drinking vodka at 9am. And despite their best efforts to sip it, their Russian counterparts kept getting them to down the stuff. We lost the game, but it didn't matter. This was an amazing event, heavily backed by the Russians, with us handing out rugby balls, even being asked to sign them.

I spooned one kick early on and got a standing ovation from the partisan crowd, but to be named man of the match and given a new telly was a bit much. I had not thrown the game and didn't play that well. I am sure they thought it was a bung. It was a huge TV too.

After the match I ran into a guy, a Russian, who was Pototski's sort of understudy and he was very officious and began shouting at the players to get ready for the dinner event.

There I am telling him to get stuffed and leave us alone as the lads wound down, but he kept shouting in bad

English for us to get ready. We were toe-to-toe when Pototski came in and I looked at him and understood to back down. He sent the guy away. He had a way of doing that with just a stare. Impressive I thought.

The afternoon post-match dinner was an enormous event with Davison and Fothergill on the top table still slugging back the vodka. I remember looking at Davison, who sort of nodded to me as if to say 'keep and eye on us up here'. They were toasting everything and you could see our guys were leathered.

Chris presented General Vladamir Popovkin with a bottle of scotch we had taken over and did a small talk about the tour and so on, before things got really messy. I remember after the event we were heading back to the hotel with plans for an evening event. I saw Smalesy wearing the general's fur (ushanka) hat on the steps outside. They were all battered, arms round each others shoulders, laughing and merry, very merry. By 6pm everyone was in a terrible state. I made a decision, along with a guy called Tony Holmes, that the guys should not go out, rather stay in the hotel bar and carry on drinking. This caused some upset, but I didn't want guys waking up in jail or the middle of nowhere, so Fothers gave out the order and a few of us attended the evening event.

My guess was right and I ended up preventing a scene between 'Spider' James Le Mar and Fothers. Le Mar, a massive prop forward, was drunk as a lord and saying he wanted to deck Fothers. In my other ear I had Fothers saying; 'Le Mar wants to deck me. I could get him arrested.'

We had escaped without too much incident. I was glad the lads had returned, I didn't want this to be like a union tour, which seem to attract bad publicity.

There was one incident that almost resulted in us attracting a bit more attention than would have been desired when we were invited to the air attaché residence near Red Square. The lads were in buoyant mood. We knew things were a massive success. The attaché told us he had been involved in more commerce since we had arrived than in the previous three years he had been posted to the country, and that the evening he put on was in the main part to celebrate that fact.

I arrived with eight of the other lads, including Fothers, 'Spider' and Gary Bamford. We were in great spirits and piled into the tiny lift that serviced the building, ignoring the sign that clearly pointed out 'maximum load five persons' (even though it was in Russian, the symbols are international). Any lift would struggle with eight heavily built rugby lads and this one was no exception. It ground to a halt a few floors up. At which, we all began giggling like very cramped school kids, until Fothers began to panic that is, after what seemed like just a few seconds. He began to claw at the doors, forcing them open slightly, and yelled: 'HELP! HELP US! WE ARE TRAPPED IN HERE!'

Frankly, it was a bit embarrassing. We didn't know he was claustrophobic and the lads didn't really take it seriously at all, cracking jokes as Fothers continued to lose the plot.

I kept telling him to calm down, but 'Spider' and the lads were having a ball. Then the big man turned to Fothers and suggested that, with our weight, we should all jump up in the air and unwedge the obviously stuck lift, causing it to start again.

We were all biting our lips as Fothers, now sweating, agreed. After about five or six attempts to free the lift and howls of laughter, we were still jammed in.

Then one of the lads suggested Fothers rang for help. They gave him Gary's mobile number, but in his chaotic mindset, he had forgotten that Gary was stood behind him.

Muttering to himself, Fothers dialled the number with shaking fingers and we watched on in silence, with bated breath.

'Right,' he said, placing the phone firmly to his ear. He didn't even notice the ring tone of Gary's phone behind him. 'Ah, Gary', he said, before Gary replied: 'Yes, mate?'

Cue more howls of laughter. We were stuck in there for about 25 minutes, but it took longer than that for the story to stop being told.

At the airport, preparing to depart, I learned a valuable lesson about people. I had been chatting with Pototski's number two. With things calmer, he asked about our wage structures at work, discovering he would never earn the wages we did and so on. It was an eye opener, but so was the fact that he gave me a leather-bound, over-the-shoulder map holder. It was a lovely thing and not cheap. He would have nothing of it, it was his honour to give it to me. I was stunned. Friendships had been built; there was no question of that.

Financially, we are not in a position to invite the Russians over to England, but we had done our bit over there. Rugby league had built a new bridge and we had played our part in the sport's history. I would love our paths to cross again one day. Maybe this time I could turn their room over.

# The Battle of Wounded Knee

*22 September 2006*

*In rugby league history: 22 September (2012): USA Tomahawks defeated Canada Wolverines 36-18 in Fairford, Conneticut, in the third Annual 1812 Colonial Cup fixture.*

*In RAF history: 22 September (1943): Bomber Command carried out the first 'spoof' raid technique when the primary target was Hanover. Twenty-one Lancasters and eight Mosquitos of No.8 Group carried out a diversionary raid dropping much Window and many flares and target indicators to simulate a larger force attacking Oldenburg.*

ALTHOUGH not some old sage or storyteller myself, I have begun to realise how life sometimes plays strange hands that then see you going in the right direction.

The fickle finger of fate and so on, some might call it, but to think that a bad injury, well one of the worst any sportsman can suffer, would eventually lead me to the right place in my sporting career is unusual to say the least.

## The Battle of Wounded Knee

The injury? Snapping my ACL (Anterior Cruciate Ligament) as I dived for a try in the opening Inter-Services clash against the Royal Navy at Burnaby Road.

There are a few things that stick in the mind: how well I was playing, how I didn't believe I had hurt myself so badly and how much it hurt. Add to that the ribbing I have received over the years whenever the video footage is shown of my reaching out a hand to Jason Talbot who had run over to help me. It looks like I am asking him to hold my hand, when in truth I was asking for a hoist up, but the bastards won't ever let me get away with it.

The final game had been coming. Not that I had been playing wildly or taking risks, but internally I had found myself becoming more and more involved in the wider parts of the game, talking with higher ranking officers about where we should take it, rubbing shoulders with icons of the sport and generally thinking how I would need to hand over the captain's armband so rugby league could move forward, fresh starts etc. I had found that before the injury my focus was on the 80 minutes, pure and simple, short to mid-range focus. But since I began looking to the future, relationships with senior management became stronger. I was changing and so was the game around me. I didn't want to get left behind and somehow the injury had ensured that I wouldn't.

I will come back to that, but thinking of the first steps towards this new world, the biggest one came in November 2005 when I first met a man who can only be described as a rugby league icon , then Australia national team coach Wayne Bennett. Funny to think that a chance meeting would end up with a friendship or at least a mutual respect that has grown ever since, so much so that we have met and spoken on many occasions. He is a man who is always worth listening to.

Our first meeting came after Graham Clay, conduit

between the RFL and Gillette's sponsorship of the sport, had been in touch. He was looking for extra-curricular activities for the Australian team who were to take part in the Tri-Nations (Australia, New Zealand and Great Britain) event of that year. I jumped at the chance and began organising some events at RAF Linton-on-Ouse. There I am, an FS, working with the best team in the world - get in! I thought this would be a one-off, so I got on the team coach and started handing out marker pens and balls, getting them to sign them and posing in photographs, the lot. A proper tourist I was. Well why not? How did I know how well this relationship would go? I dared not imagine.

I was still thinking with a short-term mentality.

Well it couldn't have gone any better. Scrum-half Craig Gower was taken flying and Sky Sports were all over it. I got to spend quality time with Bennett, unreal. Things got better when Graham, under a request from the Australian team, invited us to attend that year's Golden Boot event at Elland Road, Leeds. So there we were, myself and my builder mate Mark Gear sat with players such as Darren Lockyer and Danny Buderus in our penguin suits, being filmed on Sky TV. The best players in the world and us; it was mad.

I had my medals on, you are allowed to wear them at events such as that, and I recall Bennett giving Mark some right shit about what he was doing there, friendly but funny. They seemed cool with me, but were giving him a terrible ribbing. It was a great night and a friendship had been struck up with one of the legends of the game. How good is that?

Another stand-out moment, which saw me building bridges and expanding the game for the Service, was the arrival of GB captain Paul Sculthorpe to RAF Marham, 31 Sqn, which was overseen and organised by Deano. Scully and me are now good pals and that day saw the GB skipper and

RAF captain take to the air in RAF Tornados. It was a brilliant event and once again Sky covered it extensively.

I was helping facilitate the event and began to feel more at home doing this side of things. Scully is a top lad and an outstanding player who had already won back to back Man of Steel honours. I met him the night before and he kipped in the Sergeants' Mess. I took him into the Mess bar and we were having a few beers. I just sat and watched as people began to recognise him and came over asking for autographs and posing in photographs with him. It was amazing and I had helped organise that. It was a different feeling from kicking a goal or making a tackle (which didn't happen too often), but it was almost as good. I could see the real benefits for the sport as a whole.

My relationship with Deano was growing as well and it has done since I stopped playing really. It's gone from strength to strength. The moment you injure yourself badly always stays with you and, in a funny way, it came just as I was reaching my peak, fitness wise.

I had gone from being stationed at Halton to being posted to Banja Luka in Bosnia as part of Op OCULUS. My role was (MTO) Mechanical Transport Officer, as part of an Army detachment 36 at the time. I was deployed in August 2006, but was allowed to return for the Inter-Services in September of that year. There is really only one way to describe Banja Luka and that is unfinished; some bits are really grand others half built or just crumbling.

We were only allowed restricted access outside the camp, but I clearly remember seeing families roasting whole pigs on a spit on their driveways; they were hard-looking bastards as well. The deployment was what is known as 'Out of Area' for four months, at the back end of the conflict. Within a year of my return the whole place was shut down.

## Through Adversity

It was mainly an Army base and we were housed in the Banja Luka metal factory, which was exactly that and had dozens of sheet metal presses dotted around. It was a bit like Sheffield in that way. We had a fleet of 175 vehicles, from DAF four-tonners to cars, and we were providing full vehicle support. It was an established area, with a few Dutch air force guys out there and one RAF guy alongside me, Cpl John Millard. We were shacked up in Corimec accommodation, which is basically like a Portakabin, and it is shared.

The atmosphere was fairly volatile, with a mix of religious beliefs, and our presence provided a large chunk of the local income, but you never really felt safe. It reminded me of Belfast in that way. Certain areas were beautiful, fabulously green and untouched. Sarajevo was a stunning city but, of course, it had been affected by the conflict, so large chunks were ruined. As I said, we weren't allowed out that much, large areas were mined, so you couldn't go off-piste as it were. It was something of an eye-opener and, sadly, it will probably be that way forever.

I met some really good guys such as Andy Dobbie and Lego, and there were a lot of reservists. It was also very interesting to see how the Army worked. But there was nothing to do. We simply got up, worked and went down the gym. It was all you could do to prevent boredom setting in.

I had already been toying with the idea of handing over the captaincy. I was fitter than I had ever been, for the reason just stated, so going into the games I sort of fell on my sword. The armband was given to Martin Wood, who would also play at stand-off, which also enabled me to play with a bit more freedom. He would be taking the kicks, with that unusual style of his. Anyone who has seen him kick knows what I mean. And I thought I was playing really well in the usual heated atmosphere of Burnaby Road. We were leading and eventually went on to win the title. I had just put in a kick and was running for the try-line when two Navy players hit me from either side and snap, searing pain, then nothing for a few seconds. I had no idea how bad it was, so much so that I got bandaged up and went back on collecting the ball and falling on my arse as I tried to jink inside. It was agony and that, as they say, was that.

Wood won the man of the match and I was delighted for him. The Navy chairman kindly said a few words about how Wood had: 'Big boots to fill' and in truth he had stepped up well and is a very good player and kicker. I was delighted for him, so I drove home to Halifax the next day still thinking about playing and getting fit for the Army game that was coming up.

I stopped off on the way to get some flowers for Lorraine. Well, it was our wedding anniversary, so what nicer way to celebrate than by spending hours in A&E in agony with a knee the size of a football? I couldn't even get out of the car, the sales girl had to bring them to me. Still, not believing I was that badly hurt, I went to see a doctor at RAF Uxbridge the following Monday, then eventually went to Headley Court, near Dorking, as part of the Elite Sportsman programme the Service provides.

Due to the swelling I was out of the Army match, but still kept thinking: 'Oh it's not that bad'. I needed to return to Bosnia and was apprehensive about doing so, as I was injured and they had been so good to let me take time off, but I got back. The swelling went down a bit and I just got on with things. The injury allows you to do that. You can use your leg, just not for anything other than walking around.

Then, in January the following year, I was stationed at RAF Aldergrove. I was an FS still for MT, but I was no longer an instructor and given a slot for my operation in

## Through Adversity

Belfast. At least they should know how to repair knee injuries properly with the amount of kneecapping that went on in the area, I thought. So there I was all gowned up counting to two and waking up with a new knee. My beloved sport followed me everywhere and still does. I clearly remember being told to stay in bed, but noting that the Super League was on the TV I used a bit of Clayton charm to get the nurses to allow me to get up and watch it. I lasted ten minutes. The pain was so bad I was nearly sick and passed out.

Aldergrove was a good Station experience for me, I honestly didn't know what to expect. Op BANNER was still in progress due to the ongoing conflict over the Northern Ireland situation, so I was apprehensive. The Station itself was a tight little place, not many RAF sports or any sports went there due to its position to the north of Belfast. Other stations couldn't be bothered to go over. So any sporting endeavours you offered to start up were fully supported, hence when I pushed for league to be played there, well I got full backing.

Aldergrove Storm was formed in 2008 and we shone in the RAF Cup, making the final that year, losing to Marham, and then winning the bloody thing in 2009, beating Benson. It was the last final held at Uxbridge and part of it was the final months of the Station, not only for me but also for itself, as 230 Sqn moved to Benson with the Station closing in September to become Joint Helicopter Flying Station Aldergrove.

We took advantage of the Station's lack of interest from other sporting quarters to tie in with the professional side of rugby league and this began when Graham Clay, then Chief Executive of Halifax RLFC, got in touch wanting to do something different for a training and team-building exercise for the club's pre-season preparations.

As part of the exercises we had organised for them we held a TAB, Tactical Advance to Battle, which saw the lads get up really early and we bussed them to the far side of the Station's airfield, with walking stretchers and half-filled jerry cans. The idea of a TAB is that teams, which they were split into, have to make their way intact to an area and then fight. They made their way through the dark and just as they got close to the coaches, 100 yards away, we made the coaches pull away. This is the critical moment when people learn about each other and who is a team player and who lifts the people around them.

We had the team for three days, Friday to Sunday, and the next day I gave them a talk about Op TELIC. There I was showing the players DVD of our helicopters and jets carrying out bombing raids and everybody was loving it, except one guy. I found out he was a French Muslim. To say I learned from that lesson is an understatement.

The unknown factors that remain as such in sporting teams and groups was highlighted when we sat the guys in groups to just talk and one guy revealed he had a brother serving in Afghanistan. He told how he was worried about his brother a lot of the time and the players realised that at times when he was down they had no idea why. They just thought he was being moody, but now they knew and it would help them in the future and with other players as well.

Another memory that sticks was when I got the guys to carry out 'Trust Falls'. These do exactly what they say on the tin and require a lot of faith in your colleagues. I had Chf Tech Lee Dunn along to help out and we put the guys through it.

You have to take the rough with the smooth in life and that year marked a few highs as well as lows, the high for me being winning the Combined Services Official of the year award. It was another step up the ladder for the sport as CS awards are important for the RAF. They host the event at the RAF Club in Piccadilly every year but hardly ever win anything, it does seem unfair. I had an inclination that I had won beforehand as Air Marshal Peach, our President, had indicated he would not be able to attend, being a very busy man, unless I had won. So I was quietly confident when I saw him arrive. I was superbly well supported by RAF Sports Board Director Chris Davison, present along with Air Marshal Peach, Lorraine and Connor. It proved a very emotional and funny day for my young lad.

For the lunch they served gazpacho to start and I noted Connor looking around confused. Davison bless him, such a lovely man, said: 'Here Connor is your soup cold?' Bless his little socks, Connor said: 'Yes.' So Davison replied: 'It's not on, they could serve warm soup ... anyway just leave it.' Connor stills gets tickled about that to this day. What a lovely thing for Chris to do though, a true gent.

Later, when they read out the citation, Connor got really upset. I don't know if it was pride, but he was sobbing bless him. That's my boy.

For me, the whole thing was something or nothing really. It was great to win an award, but it was mainly about raising the profile of our sport. So to see a second rugby league name on the trophy, that of Wayne O'Kell, who had won it two years before, was great. Two of us on the trophy, that really made me smile.

I was now set on a team management role, the penny had dropped after the knee injury. I was championing the sport and I know that I would not have achieved the things I had if I had stayed on the pitch. Every cloud and all that I suppose. I had gone from talking about tactics to strategies.

One example of the work I was able to do was with

the Schools Championships event, which we held at RAF Uxbridge for the first time in August 2007. It is the largest sports event in the world. In 2011, 1,678 teams took part, with 27,537 youngsters taking to the field.

We hosted the finals day event, as Andy Harland, the RFL School Competition's then-organiser, had approached me. I began pulling a few strings, calling in a few favours. I initially saw it as a great opportunity to sell the RAF brand, but nobody in the careers department seemed interested. Why not, I thought? Hundreds of youngsters who may be interested in the Service were there at the career department's disposal, but I kept getting bumped off.

Mark Bean and his guys from Lossiemouth (RAF) came down to help run the event, with Andy Smales overseeing proceedings as I was away and unavailable. But the aggravation of trying to get anyone interested was too much.

I have in the intervening years driven to pick up climbing walls, set up lights and banners and so on because nobody else outside the sport was interested. We stopped hosting the event when Uxbridge closed in 2010 and, in truth, looking back now, I would not even mention the words rugby league if I was selling it to the career people again. I would quote numbers and attendances and TV coverage, but not rugby league. How sad is that?

You see it seems obvious that it was not 'their' sport. I am sure if I had mentioned the other code they would have jumped at it. So I knew that the fight had to go on and I knew what my role was in that fight now.

As always, Per Ardua for rugby league.

# Jamaica Rum

*20 November 2008*

*In rugby league history:* 12 November (1926): St Helens beat arch rivals St Helens Recs by 10 points to 2 at Wilderspool, Warrington, to win the Lancashire Cup for the first time. It was St Helens's first major trophy triumph.

*In RAF history:* 20 November (1936): The RAF's first monoplane heavy bomber, the Fairey Hendon, entered service with No.38 Squadron.

WHEN you look at athletes like Usain Bolt and Asafa Powell, where they were trained, produced almost, and their amazing achievements, you begin to understand the true power of sport. I had tasted this on some tours, but during our tour to Jamaica in January 2008 I would see, first-hand, sport's true ability to improve and impact on people's lives.

In some ways, RAF sport became inextricably linked with the two runners, or at least the training camp in

Kingston where they both learned how to become world beaters, which is what we went on to become later that year as well.

Yes, 2008 was something special for all involved in RAF rugby league. We really had scaled a mountain and left an ensign planted firmly on top.

We were invited to Jamaica through the RFL. It seemed nobody cared about the efforts of the Jamaican RL set-up, who wanted to get themselves representation in the World Cup due to be played in Australia that November.

I was very conscious of the good PR we could gain for our hosts through a tour and we began in-depth contacts with the British Police, who had visited there the previous year. Deano and myself were right behind the event. From a personal point of view this was the first tour I would be completely involved in and, in many ways, the two matches played against the Jamaican Defence Force and the Jamaican national side (winning both 33-16 and 32-24 respectively at the Up Park Camp, Kingston, Jamaica) were not important, it was the wider picture that mattered.

That picture would see us benefit personally, the sport gain another feather in its cap and the hosts set themselves up for the biggest event in the sport down under.

We had changed the world of rugby league forever with the tour to Russia, now we had gone from the freezing streets of Moscow and the Forbidden City to the gun-toting, sunshine-bathed streets of Jamaica.

It was nothing if not a steep learning curve, which started at home trying to get the bloody thing off the ground. Too many people could not see the value but, luckily for us, the Service DSB Chris Davison could.

The sport itself had been taken to Jamaica by a southerner of all people, Paul Morris, himself ex-Service

(Army), who had gone to live out there. The set-up was severely lacking in funding and organisation. Morris talked a good game, but the truth was someway short. However we thought it would be good preparation for our Challenge Cup efforts. Due to Operations and money we struggled to take out a full-strength squad, but we were fully aware of giving something back as in value for money, we always have been. We put our bid in for the tour, unlike some other sports, but sometimes because we are so good with our money we can be punished by the Sports Board or those who held the purse strings. One example that springs to mind is with strapping. We would always bid for £200 a year for strapping but sourced it elsewhere, so the money would not be used. As we did this, that money was taken away from our budget, much like councils do each year. It was a case of if you have not spent it, then it was taken away.

This was purely good housekeeping as I see it and, of course, when our contact or source can no longer supply us for free, we lose out completely. I had a few ding-dongs with Cath Kelly from the RAF Sports Board. I was basically told: 'If you have it, spend it,' which seems mad to me. There has to be a purpose behind things and we never want people to use money for the sake of it.

This tour was the same. We wanted to give something back and the guys were expected to pay out towards the tour, in a year when they knew the World Cup was coming.

It is only ethically right to do this. The players must contribute, even if only because by doing so it means they have more of a personal involvement in the tour. It's about core values. You have to earn your brass, and we believe it's important for this to happen.

In many ways I could relate to the position of Jamaica in the world of rugby league, to ourselves in the Service. We helped tie our tackle shields to posts before games because they had no post protectors. We brought nothing back, left it all, and this was the centre where Bolt and Powell trained to become world-beaters. They had nothing.

A single RAF gym has tons more equipment, but in Jamaica they produce winners and I can relate to that, poor relations that come away with the silverware. It is funny how some things mirror others.

We flew out for a week and roomed together. I shared with Deano, but I was missing the camaraderie only players experience. It was very difficult. I hated not training with the lads. Having been in to give the lads a bit of a gee up before one game I was wandering about outside kicking my heels. 'Spider' Le Mar was team captain and he got the lads to look at me milling around and used me, looking lost, as an example of what it meant not to be involved and playing.

He was right, I was lost and it hurt. I was no longer standing shoulder-to-shoulder; no longer part of the 17, and that was the key. From Brighouse on, all those days in the street, all those dreams, kicking practice, tackling, journeys in mum's Mini, watching the professionals and aspiring to be like them, copying moves ... it all revolved around crossing the whitewash and being in the side.

I was no longer the Damian Clayton I knew in many ways; the lad for whom rugby league had helped keep him going when his father left.

The sport had meant I wasn't alone in those dark times. It had given me a purpose and made me the man who went to the Houses of Parliament, travelled the world, found his soul mate and fell in love, due in a large part to our shared affection for our glorious sport.

That Damian Clayton was gone and would not be coming back. Standing outside on that sports field in Jamaica, that feeling, the acknowledgement, the realisation really hit home. I was finally alone. It is OK saying a few words to people before a match or at half-time, but it was showing it on the pitch that mattered most, well at least to me.

When we had lost Jack Wilson, it was not words said at half-time when the news came through that helped me inspire and be inspired by my team-mates. It was actions on the pitch ... keeping my nerve to kick that vital point to draw the match. That was what I was about and that was what I had lost and would never be able to find again. Although my views were changing, I had already decided to move aside, even before the injury, when I returned home after the tour. I understood a new value to my involvement. At the time it was very strange and standing out there was a very lonely moment in my life.

It's been six long years since I have played at that level. I didn't know at the time how to deal with not being involved, in many ways I still don't. Not like an addict trying to stay clean, well in many ways yes I suppose it is, but it's not really the buzz I was missing, that hit addicts require. It was the whole thing and I still struggle to this day to combat that loss, to fill that space, that need.

I remember two years ago at Burnaby Road having my shorts, stockings and boots on to help out by the side of the pitch and O'Kell had to do a double take. He thought I was playing and Molly was going to send me on.

The sport was something that had in many ways been the glue that had bonded my life together through thick and thin, and a lot of thin if truth be known. The playing aspect of that had gone. Strange times indeed.

I often ask myself would I trade what I have learned and experienced since my injury for one more crack on the pitch and the only answer I came up with is that the sport needs to move on and so do I, so things are where they are for a reason. That is probably why when I was given the captaincy for the GB Masters versus Australia Masters game at Mayfield in Rochdale in July, 2010, it meant so much.

I am proud to have grown up side by side with my sport. I still play, if not to the standard I would like. But to have had the recent chance to regain a bit of pride on the pitch was a real win-win, as it all is if I am honest.

Off the pitch the Jamaica tour was nothing short of immense. I learned a lot about the aspects and the importance of being in charge, of my role, of the new Damian Clayton.

We had brought a referee from England, Peter Brooke, who was the RFL referee development officer. He couldn't believe what was going on. He nearly ran to the airport and buggered off home after the first day. There we were, walking to the training session and our game with Jamaica Defence Force at the legendary Eden Park, when laid on the road was a dead body, our first experience of life over there. The guy had been a burglar and somebody had shot him during the night and left his corpse in the road. Brooke went white with shock.

Going out, we had to get people to 'buddy up' for their own safety. Our first experience of Kingston's nightlife was when we were surrounded by armed JDF guys, being driven to a bar. When we arrived there was another bloke dead on the floor outside the nightclub. Forensics were there, white line around the body and so on. The guards made us stay on the bus until they were sure that the area was safe.

Then they took us into this club that had hardcore porn on big screens all round the place and it was full of prostitutes. One girl spent the night trying to chat up poor old Chris Davison. His face was brilliant. He was the perfect gent, obviously, not interested in her wares. He was polite all the way down the line.

## Through Adversity

We undertook a coaching session with children the following day, where the pitch was surrounded by armed JDF guards, it was an amazing experience. It was very productive overall, though, especially as we were also hosted at the High Commission by the Defence Attaché.

On the home front, we ended up with the wooden spoon in the Inter-Services. Even though the matches were close, we lost - which although disappointing was deflected somewhat by our heavy involvement in organising and preparing for the World Cup, where I took an active decision to keep away once the event started. I had toured for the last four years or been busy, so I wanted to be on holiday with my family. I was in Australia catching games and keeping in touch with the lads, but was ostensibly on holiday, even though I learned a massive lesson while there about missed opportunities.

Having been aware to some degree that we had missed out on media coverage in Jamaica, it literally slammed me in the face after the Armed Forces World Cup, which ran side by side with the professional event.

My family had travelled over there with Graham Clay and his family and I was attending events alongside him, seeing how the players were greeted by local dignitaries, touching base and forming relationships with people like Jamie Peacock and other players and coaches.

I still became a point of contact for anyone trying to find out information on Service matches. It was not on really. I didn't mind fielding the calls, but it was just not up to scratch and we achieved so much, only for so few to find out about it.

I was taking calls from the RFL asking me about results of matches in the Service World Cup. The player preparation was second to none, but nobody else knew about it. Why ring me? I was on holiday.

I vowed when the RAF went to Australia in 2009 that it wouldn't happen again and it didn't.

In part a lot of this has to do with my relationship and friendship with Sgt Richard 'Sponge' Beattie, whom I first met at Aldergrove back in 2007. Sponge is an infectious lad, and now a good friend and has helped us really sell the brand of RAF rugby league, taking it to a new audience through his superb photographs. I originally encountered him when he came along to play for the Storm. He played prop in union, but tried out for us. Although, to be fair, he could only muster up one big drive and was knackered, he is such a positive guy to have around it was great.

We got chatting one day about him being involved in the RIGC (Regional Intelligence Gathering Centre) and being a photographer and he agreed to help me put together some images for posters to get the team started.

It was then that the penny dropped. I thought we were really missing a trick with this guy, so I asked him to help us out as a photographer. We now have the best images in the Service, a full library of images for all sections of RAFRL, which is superb.

If anyone knows Sponge's size, they will understand what I mean when I say that to us he really is worth his weight in gold. We joke that he once spotted somebody touching his buffet plate, which he had left in the dug-out during a 9s tournament in York, from 40 yards.

Through our growing contacts we have been able to help Sponge self-actualise as he now takes shots for the RFL at Grand Finals and Wembley. For the World Cup, the guys had prepared so well, they were pushing the boundaries on fitness, rehydration, player analysis … it was brilliant.

For the Service to have Dale Jinks win player of the tournament and have lots of RAF personnel, such as Jimmy

Through Adversity

Bardgett, all involved was excellent, surely our greatest achievement to date.

On his return, O'Kell was asked to give a presentation to the RFL Council on the preparation conducted for the GB Armed Forces team. Every professional club's chairman was present and they were all saying how much more 'professional' than them we were. It was a massive compliment to the lads and the Service as a whole.

It really had gone full circle. The Military had taken the game to the world originally, now we were the touchstone in many ways for the professional game, having won the Armed Forces World Cup. It was a great accolade and a great position to be in. Further accolades were bestowed on the association indirectly with Deano being awarded an OBE and Air Marshal Peach a Knighthood, in January 2009, making it one of the standout periods since we began and one of immense pride.

Another of those standout moments was being reacquainted with Wayne Bennett, and the organisation of a mock-up photograph of the squad at Sydney Cricket Ground. It was so important for me to do that.

Every GB Lions tour since the 1930s has posed in a picture like that in front of the main pavilion and although the historic significance may have been lost on some of the lads. It was an important moment to realign us with our sport, to be part of that tradition. We were representing our country in the sport of our choice. My Air Force and my sport were doing things how they were supposed to be done.

I have seen the Service's union sides posing in front of Sydney Harbour Bridge in pictures from their tours down under, that has no history. The SCG picture we had shows tradition.

Our tradition.

# Landing Down Under

## 22 June 2009

*In RAF history:* 22 June (1999): Operation Allied Force; following the termination of the operation, the Harrier and Tornado detachments returned to their home bases in the UK. A force of six Harrier GR7s remained in theatre to support NATO ground forces if required.

THE Australia tour was typical of RAF rugby league's history thus far, as in it was created and conducted through adversity and although we achieved great things, the starting point could not have been any more shocking if it had tried.

There had been a change in the command structure of the team back in 2008 when Andy Smales had stood down from the post of head coach, after he was told of an imminent posting to Cyprus.

This in itself should not really be a problem for any sporting association and it wasn't. Smales's assistant, possibly the most experienced and decorated rugby league man in our Service, Sgt Dave Moll, stepped in to his shoes and all should have been rosy.

Dave had a great pedigree, he was the only one of us to have played professionally, taking to the field for Keighley and Halifax. He also played GB U23s, where his captain was the legendary Brian Noble. And despite starting off losing the Inter-Services, he was more than capable of the job. Dave is a thinker, he is very calm in his ways as a coach, very hands off. He just tweaks things here and there, a watcher you might say.

Coming from Drighlington, Leeds, and with his experience, people may expect him to be a bit more of a bawler and shouter. But he isn't and his approach proved valuable for us in some changing times during his tenure as coach. So it was a massive shock when two weeks before we were set to leave for Australia I received a call from Dave's wife, Dawn, on May 31, 2009, saying: 'Dave won't be able to make the tour Damian. He's just had a heart attack and died on the operating table at the hospital.' They revived him, but Jesus what a shock. I clearly remember saying to Dawn: 'Sod Australia, is he alright?' or words to that effect.

We knew due to the World Cup and work commitments, plus the cost of touring in general, that we wouldn't be able to take a strong squad, so we had spoken at close quarters about selecting a squad for the future, to give the lads going a real opportunity and something they would learn from.

As the Officer In Charge (OIC) of the tour, I had really grabbed the organisation by the horns. I wanted it to be a real success and had built the thing around the world-famous State of Origin series, with the aim of catching a match, along with hooking up with Wayne Bennett. These were things the lads would never forget, but to have to find a new head coach and, of course, worrying about Dave's overall health, well I hadn't bargained for that.

It is safe to say we had discussed many things about the tour, but did not have a contingency plan for the big man having a heart attack.

I had organised the link-up with Wayne Bennett during the Rugby League World Cup in 2008. Even though I was on holiday, I was still working in reality. I was fully aware that you have to take every chance that you can, make the most of every opportunity. Whether I am at Wembley or wherever, watching matches, I always look for ways to help make new contacts or extend relationships, using the situation that I have been placed in.

So there I was at the semi-final of the World Cup having gleaned an access all areas pass via Graham Clay, making my way into the triumphant New Zealand dressing room after their win against England. It makes me laugh now when I think about it, but Bennett, who gained the moniker 'Supercoach' for Australia, was assisting the Kiwi side. I just sat at the back and waited watching this amazing scene of jubilation, until Bennett saw me. When he did, he came straight over and started chatting to me about things and I mentioned his offer of tying up while we were in Oz.

It was very surreal. Nobody minded me being there and Bennett agreed to sorting stuff out. I was purely there for the lads I can tell you that. I was determined to make this happen.

This tour was going to leave no stone unturned in my pursuit of excellence, so I was delighted when he agreed to sort things out, what a great thing to agree to do.

A moment that sticks with me in that sweaty dressing room was while the players were jumping up and down and celebrating, the eight players who had not taken to the pitch were being put through their paces, and I mean battered, in a training session. One half of the room was partying, the other in a seriously tough work-out. I remember Bennett telling me: 'Their mates have been through it on the pitch, so they are going through it now.' That stuck with me and I thrived on the whole experience of being there and sealing a deal with Bennett that would prove to be so important.

AVM Davison was supporting us on the tour. It would be a swansong for him as he was due to retire later that year and, as none of us was officer rank, it was great to have 2 star recognition with us. It would mean they, the Australian Air Force, would reciprocate and it helps open more doors and raises the profile of the tour. The concerns over Dave subsided as he battled on. It was going to be difficult without him in Australia, but his assistant Jason Talbot would move into the role, which meant Woody the captain would have to step up to the plate. Plus we also had the old ship mate Dave Mortimer, who had toured Australia before, to lend a hand. I made the decision to make Dave my assistant OIC, just to make things a bit more official.

Things had sort of fallen into place after that. Woody had been given an online blog to post for *The Times*; I was delighted with that after the communications issues of the previous tours. A very generous donation of £3000 from Liz Matkin from the Co-Op, who sponsor the RL Championship, also helped to ensure a smoother experience. I had a good rapport with Liz, so that generosity was another boost to me in organising the tour.

On arrival down under, we were greeted at Randwick Barracks in a suburb of Sydney that would be our home for the next three weeks.

The facilities were incredible and our hosts could not have been any better to us. We had a swimming pool and fabulous gym facilities and sat down upon arrival to discuss the ways we could really utilise what was on offer.

We had agreed to train as much as we could, and also having been told that the professional game had been taking a bit of a battering due to lots of bad press, that we would set a good example and create some interest in our being there. The tour had a more fluid feel to it, so having trained at the barracks and then played our first game there against the Australian Navy, losing 18-10, we decided to take part in a training session at nearby Coogee Bay. That created some good interest, with a lot of locals coming along to watch and interact with us.

If I think about those opening matches and sessions it's a miracle we got to do them at all after Shippers intervened and began organising things. The old sea dog began taking charge within a few hours of our arrival: 'I know how this place works Damo' and so on. 'Stick with me, I will sort it all out.'

He began putting the kit away and left a lot of stuff outside the rooms, such as balls and tackle shields. I clearly remember asking if he was going to put them away, only to be told in no uncertain terms: 'No need ship mate, I know these people everything will be fine.' We went out for a few beers and a wind down after our long haul flight only to return and all the stuff was gone. Three hours we had been there and we had to go cap in hand to the RAAF to ask for some more balls and so on. Bloody Shippers. Alan Whicker he wasn't; international man of travel my arse.

The first signs of things being wrong came about during what should have been a stand-out moment.

We were set to play in the curtain-raiser match for the NRL fixture of St George Illawarra Dragons and Queensland Cowboys at the WIN Stadium in Wollongong.

## Through Adversity

We were facing the Australian Air Force and blew it, big time. The lads really let themselves down, losing 44-16, hammered out of sight. It was embarrassing and I felt, and still do to this day, that I should have acted on the signs I had seen building between Jason and Woody.

I didn't and if I am honest that was due in part to the Alex Killen incident years before. I had changed as a person because of that and felt people had to learn from their mistakes. But I feel now, and did at the time, that I should have stepped in. I regret that.

Jason was shattered and to be honest he was ready to get on a plane and go home. The relationship between the two of them had completely broken down despite us having meetings every morning, something I call testing and adjusting, to see how things were going. The atmosphere afterwards was terrible and it took until the next match in Canberra versus a strong Australian Capital Territories side, who were an U20s feeder side for Canberra Raiders, for things to change. These kids were racing snakes and we had a depleted side not only morale wise, but in numbers. Ozzy Hicks had to take to the field, while old warhorse Clayton even had his boots on, along with a heavily strapped up knee, just in case I was needed.

It was a great game and the lads played really well, proving that through adversity we could all pull together. We narrowly lost, 32-22, but one thing that did annoy me was that I was left with the biggest pair of shorts, like a bloody skirt. The bastards stitched me up. I wasn't annoyed really, it was a right laugh, but I looked stupid.

One moment that stood out was before the game. We had a young RAF Regiment Gunner, SAC Stephen Ashcroft. He had never toured with us before, or played at senior level, and he felt close enough to the lads to stand up and give a rousing speech before we went out. It was very emotional and stayed in my memory.

It is particularly poignant because six months after that speech he was seriously injured in an IED explosion in Afghanistan.

Despite going through his rehabilitation, he won't be able to play again and it is a tragedy in more ways than one. But it was fabulous that he felt safe enough with us to express his inner-most thoughts and feel confident enough to lift us all in another dark time, admittedly not that same as he knows now, but a dark time none the less. I am sure his attitude will pull him through.

Wayne Bennett was himself struggling with things on a personal level when we arrived for our training session. A life-long friend of his had just died and he had just returned from the funeral the morning we rolled up in Illawarra.

His opening words to me were: 'Mate, I forgot you guys were coming.' That didn't stop the big man sorting us out. He was amazing and the impact that experience had on the lads was incredible, a great moment. I felt so proud to have helped to organise it.

As he was pulling his guys into shape to sort us out, I told the lads that this was a once-in-lifetime opportunity. They would be training with people like Wendell Sailor. It was important that they took as much from it as they could. Despite being the hardest 80-minute session our lads have ever had, they loved it. I swear now if we had undertaken that session before the Australian Air Force game we would have won it. The lads left the field two inches taller and I was delighted, it was very gratifying. Seven or eight of them came up to me afterwards and shook my hand and said: 'Thanks.' That meant more to me than any award I have ever been given.

Again Clayton learned things from that experience, one of the most important being during the presentation afterwards when we gave Bennett a signed, framed RAF shirt. He was delighted with it and I just wanted a bit of our history to be adorning their walls.

Then he came up to me and said: 'Tell them what you do, mate.' What he wanted was for me to tell his players what our lives were like, how some of our guys, such as Ashcroft, would be going back to Afghanistan and could lose their lives. He wanted those professional players to realise how lucky they were.

It dawned on me afterwards how the Service has been able to give things back; for professional clubs to benefit from us, from our skill sets, be it either England Elite, Halifax or the Dragons, and I was beginning to feel comfortable talking with these big names such as Wayne Bennett and Steve McNamara, the England coach. It was a bit of cometh the hour, cometh the man and I was fully recognising that and benefiting from it.

We had done a few things on the tour to help show and teach our lads not only about the game but Service life. For example, we went to the Canberra War Memorial, which was very humbling. The Anzacs did so much in the war and contributed so highly and they are rightly proud of that.

To finish the tour we took in a State of Origin game back in Sydney, which was a fantastic experience. The most intense rugby league in the world made an impression on the guys, how could it not?

I was to get a reminder of how fickle Service life can be on my return to Aldergrove though. Having organised a touring party of 32 Service personnel to the other side of the world, without a hiccup, I returned to my Station, which was undergoing a transition from RAF to Army, to find my annual appraisal giving me a kicking for not being on the ball enough in many ways and not being committed enough to my Service.

I couldn't believe it.

It read: 'As ever, he [Clayton] has maintained a very keen focus on RAF rugby league that has seen him away for a large portion of the period on a highly successful tour for which he received 2 star praise. That said, in a difficult transition as the RAF draws down from Aldergrove, his efforts would have been better placed at home.'

The large portion it mentions was three weeks of a 12-month reporting period and it really does beggar the question would this have been said if I had been heading up a tour for another sport?

I will never know, but still …

I had some sort of payback when I moved across to Cranwell, the home of officer training in the RAF, and Master Clayton had been placed at the Station as SWO (Station Warrant Officer).

The move was to be the culmination of years of planning between Deano and myself, after we knew of the potential closure of RAF Uxbridge, our home for sport at that time, a venue we shared with the football association.

Cranwell was identified as a good home because of its status. We were being more strategic and to show that we were an elite sport, what better place to have as your home than the Station that provided the RAF's elite? In truth I had been aware of the need to raise our profile from the start, but things really came home to roost a few years before when I was chatting to a PEdO who told me that the sport was not officially recognised and therefore was not represented in the Sports Board's *Coaching and Officials* book, which is published every year and means personnel can obtain training in the sport. It was little incidents like this that showed me we needed to drive things forward, to really put ourselves in the place we deserved to be.

So the first day I stepped foot on the Station also signalled the first day of the association's new home and the home of the officer cadre. To be honest, to be accepted there was a blinder, and I know the union guys feel they have missed a trick, that they should be there. We have welcomed them up there to see how we do things, and that in itself has led to them using the Station's amazing facilities to train, but it is our home.

In truth, we are very lucky to have such great support from the former and present Station Commanders, Gp Capts Dave Waddington and Nigel Wharmby, who loved the tie-in with the elite sports that we have been able to introduce when working with the England ETS & Knights and Halifax RL. It is perfectly aligned with what the Station is about.

I am always looking at ways of keeping our sport one step ahead, so it is great to have been in discussion with Deano planning our strategy; for example, we have discussed my applying for the role of Recruit Training Squadron WO at RAF Halton for a future posting, which would mean that I am the first face the Service's new young Airmen see. I could then engage with them before others do, telling them about our association and so on, hopefully signing a few up.

Until then I remained fully focused on ensuring rugby league was firmly embedded at Cranwell until the time I left in March 2012, when I was posted to RAF Coningsby.

# New Horizons

*8 March 2012*

**In rugby league history:** March (2011): Chris Thorman scored a record 56 points in a match (4 tries, 20 goals) playing for York City Knights v Northumbria University in the Carnegie Challenge Cup 3rd Round.

**In RAF history:** March (1973): Operation Khana Cascade. In the biggest airlift since Berlin, RAF Hercules transports of 46 Group drop some 2,000 tons of grain, maize and rice to Himalayan villagers in Nepal.

THE Brian Clough saying: 'It only takes a second to score a goal' is very true. Short periods of time sometimes make massive changes in life. It was certainly a short period of time that helped complete the circle of my story so far; the amount in my case being 96 hours.

That was how long I was given to prepare to head off

to Gioia del Colle in Italy as part of the RAF bombing missions to help depose Colonel Gaddafi in Libya. I was going in the role of Theatre MTO and after four months on tour the scoreline was Clayton one, Gaddafi nil, as the conflict had all but ended with the fall of Tripoli a few days before my return. It also happily coincided with the Rugby League Challenge Cup final at Wembley.

One negative, though, was leaving our Connor in the UK facing an operation for the same injury his dad had suffered, ACL reconstruction.

Hurrying around in the intervening days before my posting date of April 27, 2011, I organised a meeting with Dave Moll, Woody and Jase Talbot to discuss the coming months while I was away, which would include the build-up to the Inter-Service matches. During the meeting Dave Moll informed us that he wanted to make a sideways move out of the role of first-team coach and we agreed to this.

Dave only had two years left to serve and he had been great for us, so this was no problem at all if that's what he wanted. It would mean he was still involved to some degree. We appointed Chief Tech Mark Bean to first team manager; so I headed off to Libya thinking the future of our association was settled, little did I know how wrong I would be.

The posting gave me a sharp wake-up call when a young SAC, James Smart, was killed during a crash on a sustainment transportation run. Smart, who was only 23, was part of a 10-vehicle packet taking part in a sustainment run from RAF Wittering to Italy driving supplies, when he was tragically caught up in the fatal accident. I never dreamed I would be involved in anything like the death of a young Airman, but we were called out and made the four-hour journey to the scene of the crash in Vasto, Southern Italy. We first had to offer support to our surviving personnel and then deal with the authorities, a job which was done superbly by Wing Commander Ellie Cloke. I was then involved in the repatriation of SAC Smart's body back to RAF Lyneham. I was immensely proud of the lads who volunteered to carry the coffin onto the Hercules and feel we gave the young lad a dignified send-off.

As for being involved in rugby league, that was minimal, but one thing that did happen that kept me in contact was the arrival of Air Marshal Peach, who was the then Chief of Joint Operations. I drove to pick him up from the airport and we got a chance to talk, not only operational stuff, but a bit of league as well - it was great to see him in an operational role and outside of rugby league. He let me have it, mind, the next morning as I was helping him with his bags and negated to don my head dress. His reprimand was subtle but suitably clipped for me to know I'd been had. Great stuff!

On my return to the UK, I was greeted by a letter from Bean saying that due to his impending posting and increased workload he couldn't give the role his full attention, so another meeting was organised, this time with Deano and Chris Gordon present, along with Talbot and Woody.

We offered the role to Jason, who declined it, citing his experiences in Australia as proof to himself that he was not cut out for the role of head coach. We were all acutely aware that after the heavy defeats we had fallen to in the recent Inter-Service matches we really needed to stabilise and take a good look at ourselves.

If we hadn't been given a good thumping by the Army, a game we lost 47-14 on our way to the wooden spoon in the Inter-Services, we may have just papered over the cracks. The link between A-grade, Station and the first XIII league team really needed looking into. The preparation for the IS matches had been poor, we had really let ourselves down as an association, taken things for granted, so we were at a bit of a crossroads until Gordon piped up.

He is a very enthusiastic lad, an exceptionally gifted player and he is always looking to get involved and help organise things, especially since he suffered a bad knee injury while on tour in Afghanistan. So when he started saying there was only one man for the job, a man with the drive and ambition to really do it justice and that's Damian, I was a bit embarrassed to be honest.

I had secretly longed for the job, but had kept it to myself. After it was agreed I suggested that Chris be given the role of team manager. That way I felt I could assist and mentor him to ensure the right standards are being met. Chris has bags of enthusiasm and I see a bit of me 10 years ago in him.

If I take a step back I can really see how I am now taking the role that I so desired in my younger years, that of a father figure who can take people under his wing, guide them and ensure they are given the opportunity to bloom. I never would have thought 15 years ago that I would be doing the role that Jack Wilson did, but I am chomping at the bit. The appointment is the culmination of everything I have learned. All the knocks have led to this point and the team will, I hope, benefit from it. We had started from such humble beginnings, through to securing the placement at Cranwell.

The appointment as first team coach meant I could now give something back and, in many ways, it was the first time in four years that I had crossed the whitewash at that level, when I took my first coaching session in March 2012.

I hit the ground running, using my contacts within the game. I agreed with the governing body at Red Hall to utilise their expertise, video analysis, stuff that is proven to work in the pro' game and I wanted to introduce it into ours.

In many ways the pain in the arse that the young

Clayton had been to officers in the Service will be the same for the likes of Steve McNamara and Wayne Bennett, the only difference being they actually want to help us out so won't be annoyed by me as much, which is terrific. What other sport would that be happening in? I cannot imagine one.

The whole thing kicked off with our first round Challenge Cup match, in February 2012, followed by a tour to Canada in June that would once again see us pioneer the sport across the world, before a series of warm-up matches and then the Inter-Service clashes took place.

I had already got the wheels in motion and was keen as mustard to get started. I had helped transform my sport and it has changed me into who I am today. This is where I should be. The coaching role helped me self-actualise and it felt right. I now had the chance to impart all my experience and to instil the discipline that would help shape our players and Service personnel for the better. I was ready. I wouldn't shy away from the tough decisions either, I knew that much.

Having met up with Steve in the days leading up to the Four Nations final match against Australia (2011), at Loughborough University, Nottingham, I realised what would be expected of me. McNamara told me that he had one final tough decision left to make, to select the team to face the Kangaroos. Well, I wanted those tough decisions as well.

For Jack Wilson, now see Damian Clayton; for the father figure of Jeff Greenwood, now see Damian Clayton; for training with Nigel Marshall and Paul Nuttall, now see Damian Clayton.

For Damian Clayton standing alone at Eden Park in Jamaica, now see Damian Clayton standing united with the lads at RAF College Cranwell.

My time was here …

# Coach Clayton

*11 November 2012*

*In rugby league history:* 11 Nov (2001): Great Britain defeat Australia 20-12 in the 1st Ashes test watched by 21,758 spectators at Huddersfields Mcalpine Stadium. Paul Sculthorpe excelled for GB scoring 2 tries and kicking 2 goals.

*In RAF history:* 11 Nov (1918): At 10:45 on the morning of November 11th, the crew of a 15 Sqn RE.8 observation aircraft landed at Auchy and reported no enemy aircraft or anti-aircraft fire seen. Fifteen minutes later, Armistice with Germany was declared and the war ended.

TO PUT a full stop at the end of any chapter in your life is always odd, as things tend to unravel or end differently if pre-planned. That's how I have found things anyway, so to be given that full stop in the shape of an England call-up, of sorts, was just perfect.

That call-up came when I was chosen to hand out the medals at the final of the 2012 Autumn International Series as England took on France in the final of a three-team tournament and on Remembrance Sunday as well. What an honour, what a way to show off my Service and of course to cap a superb year.

The year 2012 was one of the most successful of my life, both at home, at work and within my beloved sport. I achieved things; dreams, aims, that I always wanted and I saw my family - in the shape of our Connor, who went off to University and was signed up by Halifax RLFC - take another pride inducing step along the road. Lorraine and I have never known such pride, such love for each other as when our little boy showed us what he is made of.

Taking that phone call from the operational staff at the RFL on the Wednesday before Remembrance Sunday, I just went about my business of discussing protocols, as the RFL had planned to use a young SAC to play the 'Last Post'. We discussed who would stand where, when the minutes silence should be observed and what about the Reveille?

I asked for the details of the SAC, so I could ensure he would be properly prepared, as it was on national television. I wanted to make sure if he needed any new bits of uniform and so on, that I could sort it for him. I was then asked: 'Was I going?'

I answered 'yes'. As part of the RFL Community Board I would be there, but also I wanted to see the lads, having been with them at the first Elite Training Squad meets held at RAF Cranwell in March 2011, with Steve McNamara. It was set to be a wonderful experience, I was buzzing about the day.

And then into the conversation was calmly slipped: 'Would you think about presenting the medals with Maurice Watkins, RFL Chairman?' I was gobsmacked, but it took me all of one second to answer. Outwardly, I was thinking, what a ribbing I am going to get, some serious abuse. There have been lots of jokes over the years about me being sat at functions and seen me sitting at matches and so on. Inside I thought 'Fecking hell, professional players, national television and me.'

The telephone went down and I sat there laughing for a while, when Tony 'Bones' Holmes walked into my office. Now Bonesey has been there since the beginning, he goes all the way back and he asked me what I was laughing at, probably thinking 'Clayton has finally lost it'. Having told him, he was delighted, chuffed to bits. In truth it wasn't just presenting the medals to England, it was the whole package and on Remembrance Sunday with everything that entails for me and the Armed Forces. It was brilliant.

The day began with Lorraine, Connor and I attending my local church in Ovenden, Halifax and then Lorraine and I heading off to the Salford City Stadium. I was playing a part in my sport, but that day really proved to me how wonderful this opportunity was. Connor was posting pictures up on Facebook with the words: 'Go on, dad!' I was proud because he was, as was Lorraine and my mum.

To be acknowledged as part of the game's make up is significant and it was nice to hear at the previous RFL Council meeting, when Deano presented to the Council on where we are as a sport in the Armed Forces and the impact the impending redundancy of the RFL appointed development officer could have.

To be discussing this shows how far we have come, that we are providing a lot of bang - for not a lot of buck - for the governing body.

I had that confirmed at the international when I bumped into Kevin Sinfield who was warming up on the pitch. Kev had just been announced as England captain and I said: 'Congratulations, Mister Sinfield'. He simply shook my hand and said: 'Congratulations, Mister Clayton!' I clearly remember feeling that I really belonged there. I was chatting to other players, nobody batted an eyelid.

The whole experience was great for the Service and association, but it left me with an impression of what life could be like after the RAF and where I fitted in with that. It was a fine end-point to a year that had started in such amazing fashion with me being appointed head coach to the RAF first XIII. I had always wanted that role and intended to bring in the things I had learned.

Having been appointed I knew I didn't want to leave any stone unturned. I had views and areas I wanted to cover and introduce, beginning with a tough opening match against East Hull in the first round of the Challenge Cup.

It seemed funny to be putting things into place from the head coach's position. We had kept Molly on as assistant with Jase Talbot now doing video analysis and I went off to have a look at East Hull in preparation for the game as they played Siddal, a very good side from Halifax.

I knew the things I had learned from being around people like Steve McNamara, who was willing and able to help me out with access to certain things. And I had been given access by him to his professional people at Red Hall, RFL's HQ on the road north out of Leeds, towards Wetherby. I had also already begun discussing things like diet with Middlesex College, so our players could work with experts and give them ownership over their personal performance and physical preparation. Things were being put into place weeks before in the changing room. I feel that rugby league is a simple sport, that we complicate it, and knew attention to detail was going to be key to our success.

## Through Adversity

I made a series of notes on what I saw in the East Hull game, which we then began to go through. There were key areas I wanted to exploit and get good at, which would stand us in good stead throughout the year. I knew there were resources that we were not utilising ... attention to detail, letting the players offer feedback, working closer together. We prepared well, despite losing massive players like Jimmy Bardgett, who had left the Service. I cannot begin to say how important he had been to us, but we needed to move one and I had been determined to bring the A-graders and seniors together, to train and so on. From that, we gained a guy called Cpl Nathan Parkin, who responded brilliantly to the opportunity that coaching afforded.

It had all stemmed from that initial morning when I walked into the changing room at Cranwell. We were there to train and I was extremely nervous, all the people who had wanted me to fail over the years, Clayton's train set etc, now was the perfect time for their wishes to come true. It really was fight or flight, but the lads came out fighting.

I knew they needed discipline. I had learned that from Wayne Bennett. His teams trained for 80 minutes in the morning and then 80 minutes in the afternoon, that's it. Same time start, not one minute later, same time finish, not one minute later. The game is 80 minutes long, so that's how long we train for. I instigated that with our lads and they hit their straps and I was not having any messing about. I drilled them and they responded to it well. They were enjoying it, so we all benefited. As things turned out, East Hull beat us, but it was a pleasing defeat if that makes sense. We had battled hard and proved our worth against one of the best amateur teams in the country.

Before taking the team to Canada for a week-long visit in the June, we had a good bit of time to work together and get the lads to understand their default position. I sent them away to get fit, there would be no room for sentiment. If they were not fit enough, they didn't play.

Albeit we were playing the national team in Canada, far from a rugby league powerhouse, we would optimise our time together. We got them training really hard, with an eye on the benefits that would come from that trip and the subsequent Inter-Services tournament in September. Having flown into Toronto, we played in the outskirts of the city, but stayed in student accommodation. It was ideal. We had two games plus lots of training, two sessions everyday. We won both games and attracted a lot of media attention for the sport, but I wasn't worried about all that. Really for me it was about prep for the IS games, with players getting a full statistic pack on their performances.

Our captain, Chris Gordon, bought into everything we did. He was superb and reacted brilliantly, speaking to all the players and encouraging everyone. It really was a great stepping stone for the Inter-Services. We played more warm-up matches, the main one being a match against Driglington on a horrible pitch on the outskirts of Leeds, against a really good side. We had a good side out, but there was no room for anyone to hide. It really was a stark reality, but they rose to it, 100 per cent, working for each other. We lost, but the result did not matter. We were going to be alright for the Inter-Services, we were going to be alright.

So it was to war and the culmination of our season. We had back-to-back fixtures so we knew what we had to do, and it all started to hit home when we traveled down to Portsmouth on the Wednesday. We had trained at Cranwell, the first two days of the week, then trained down there at Portsmouth rugby union club's ground, as all the Navy pitches were booked. But we were there, camped in, set up, the lads were in a good mood. I knew that this was the fittest squad we had ever had, plus there was a healthy competition for places, so it was all going well until we did the shirt presentation on the Friday afternoon before the game.

It was Shippers' last game and a poignant moment, there wasn't a dry eye in the house. I did my bit, talking about how important our 'family' is. We spoke of how we go through things together. There we were in the Senior Rates Mess at HMS Nelson, it was a very proud moment for Dave and for all of us and everyone was hiding their tears. All were trying to be tough and ready for the big match, well that put the kibosh on that.

It was game on after that, though, and everybody pulled themselves together except me, who was a nervous wreck under it all. I don't think I have ever been to the toilet quite so many times as I did that day. I was really grateful Dave Moll was there. He had been my leveller throughout the season, his experience as a coach as a player, as an international player ... if you took him away I would have lost my right arm.

So there we were sitting in the stand with some new communication radios. We had a man sent off, Bobby McGregor, with Garry Dunn sin-binned. I was saying 'get Jono Colley warmed up' but as I was looking another player began warming up, then another guy went on the pitch. The comms had gone out the window. I was screaming and shouting, Molly had not heard a word I said, and this was all within the first 20 minutes. I almost stormed over to the dug out, which I never like to do. We held on for 70 minutes, it was like Rorke's Drift, but the lads stood up, they were amazing. Chris Gordon had an outstanding captain's knock, scoring a trademark aggressive try, with Al Blewitt and Si Wray contributing to an amazing against all odds 19-10 win.

Mateship!

A week later, it was on to the Army game at home and a very different story. We picked up on points from the Navy game and were without McGregor on a one-match ban, but felt confident going into the game and honestly thought we would win, with a great opportunity to do so.

I had respect for our opponents, but still felt we could beat them. The half-time talk - when we were leading 20-8 - was interesting, as we spoke about being 40 minutes away. I told the lads: 'If we come off this pitch beaten and all of you can look yourself in the eye in the changing room mirror, then I don't care if we get beat.' I just wanted them to be honest with themselves, as there were players who hadn't stepped up, who hadn't played to their full potential. So I had lifted them all and, just as we were having a final gathering before leaving the changing rooms, I returned from the toilet to see Dave Mortimer in tears in the middle of the group. So they all trudged out for the second half, tears in their eyes, using their sleeves as tissues.

It was a very funny moment and pure Shippers.

I was 'thredders' at the end of that half though. We made a series of soft errors, there were decisions that went against us, but that is rugby league. We didn't lose, but we were gutted that we hadn't beaten them and the players will learn from being that close and only getting a draw.

Then it was down to Aldershot to see if the Navy could produce the goods. I felt confident. The Army had not been coached to play smart rugby. If the Navy could get at them they would win, is how I saw it. There was a strange coincidence between that game and ours against the Army, as at half-time both we and the Navy led by 12 points. I said at the time that in our game if we scored first in the second half we would put a further 50 points on them. The Navy did exactly that.

## Through Adversity

So there we were, winning the Inter Services on Army territory. It did seem just. We had such a long history with them and I was now coach. We lifted the trophy there but, for the players, it wasn't right. It should have been at home, where they could have enjoyed it properly. I felt that we were rightful winners, but it just could have been staged better for the players.

I was rightfully proud of what the lads had done and of what I had achieved in my first season as coach. In the bigger picture, it was an important win and, from a personal point of view, I had also managed to disprove the doubters.

I did have to laugh, though, when they wouldn't use my name when they presented us with the trophy.

The announcer said: 'Could a representative from RAF rugby come forward?' They knew who I was, they just couldn't bring themselves to say Damian Clayton. What's that all about? Martin Coyd who was in the stand watching sent me a text saying: 'How did the representative of the RAF feel, collecting that trophy?'

That quiet pride I had inside also came when Connor signed forms for Halifax. He is an able player who has been signed on his merits and attitude. I love watching him train and play and he is physically stronger than me, defensively as well. As a rugby league player with ball in hand, he is not quite at his dad's standard yet - but it won't be long!

It had been hard with him earlier in the year, he wasn't up to scratch with his school grades. But Lorraine and I spoke with him and invested our time, which we always do. He pulled his socks up and managed to get a rugby league scholarship at the University of Northumbria as well, so we are both really proud of him and what he has achieved, even though Lorraine is forever taking him up meals to cook. He has no idea how to look after himself like that. He might be a tough player on the pitch, but he is his mum's boy at heart. So when he signed professional forms with Halifax after getting player of the year in front of his grandparents, who are staunch Halifax fans, it couldn't have gone any better.

It was funny that Coydey and I were then asked to perform the draw for rounds one and two of the Challenge Cup in October, with Connor's team in the bag. I didn't manage to pull his side out, but how wonderful is that?

I now know that as proud as he was when he saw his dad presenting the medals at Salford, he also knows what can be achieved and what is available to him, if he puts in the effort and fights to realise his dreams.

The sacrifices are worth it, I know that all too well. You just have to keep your faith. I knew I could deliver through all the adversity, not just for myself, my family or the RAF family, but for rugby league.

# Flying High

*10 July 2013*

***In rugby league history:*** *10 July (1954): With the Ashes series tied at 1-1, Great Britain decided to rest most of their Test players and field a side which was predominantly made up of forwards for the game against New South Wales. The match was an exceptionally brutal affair, abandoned in the second half after a 26-man brawl. Great Britain lost the deciding third Test 20-16 in Sydney.*

***In RAF history:*** *10 July (1946): The Air Ministry announces that the RAF Regiment would continue as an integral part of the RAF. It would maintain rifle, armoured and anti-aircraft squadrons, and other units would be trained as airborne troops.*

I QUITE clearly remember being struck in awe, as well in no small part confused, when I heard a tale relating to the then Manchester United manager Sir Alex Ferguson, after what can only be described as the culmination of his lifetime's work after the stunning 2-1 European Cup final win in 1999.

Ferguson is alleged to have begun thinking about his next moves and conquests within five minutes of the final whistle blowing, never one to stand still and so on. And all things being relative I had a similar moment in July 2013, during my tenure as GB Lions assistant coach at the Armed Forces Rugby League World Cup in Colchester.

After chatting to some of the lads and trying to lift them following our 20-16 semi final defeat to New Zealand, I began planning for the same year's Inter-Services title defence. I also, subconsciously, did not see the point in resting or thinking too much on a situation that had passed. I do not think we should have lost and there were mistakes made from which I will learn.

For me the whole GB adventure started back in January 2012 when, not having been involved in the original World Cup triumph in Australia back in 2008, at the RFL Presidents Ball, in Leeds, with the then chairman of CS rugby league Gareth Hughes, we were discussing the World Cup and what it stood for. I had put a proposal to him regarding a team-up with myself as assistant coach, Wayne O'Kell (Navy) as head coach and Richie Nav (Army) as OIC. Wayne had finished coaching the Navy, and he was preparing for a possible future away from the Service, so once Gareth's eyes had lit up, I immediately approached Wayne to discuss him putting everything else on hold and going for this.

Wayne is one of the only people I had always wanted to work with in such a key competition. He had already got the 2008 win under his belt. I really respect him and wanted to work alongside him and see how he did business.

I am not sure if at the time my hopes may well have been to learn and then replace him after the 2013 tournament, with a possibility of reaching the peak of my career in the sport so far, but I have learned a lot more about myself and the sport I love after the Kiwi defeat, things that have taken me in a different, unseen and exciting direction.

Wayne told me, if I was committed, then he was, 100 per cent, but we needed Richie Nav onboard. And Wayne finally persuaded him late in 2012. For me, that's where it really kicked on from. To work with such key people was going to be a brilliant experience, with no stone unturned.

To have found myself in constant contact with Wayne, while working on my own first season as head coach of RAF rugby league was such an exciting time. And when Wayne finally met with Air Chief Marshal Sir Stuart Peach, Deano and the rest of key CS RL personnel in September 2012, the thing began in earnest as Wayne was effectively asked what we needed to win the World Cup.

After the IS series all three Service head coaches were asked to give a list of players they thought could make the GB squad to defend the trophy. Petty Officer Danny Johnson, SSgt Stuart Risdale and myself forwarded names and, in January 2013, 50 players were taken to Plymouth for the first of our strength and conditioning sessions with an exciting company called Kettlebell Education, run by Sam Dovey and his team.

Wayne got them involved and for me it was these extra insights and approaches that would prove interesting, exciting and educational. After all the players were assessed, they were given a 12-week S&C programme, which was worked back in detail to culminate with peak physical condition in July.

At this time I was also planning our Challenge Cup programme, which saw us battle out a tough first round match against East Leeds that we lost at Cranwell. I had only put forward 13 of our players into the GB squad, and after the East Leeds game I was even more confident that the lads chosen were more than capable of holding their own and in fact leading the charge in that environment.

Alongside Deano and Air Manning at RAF High Wycombe, we did a lot of work within the margins to ensure that key people such as Chris Gordon and Matt Watkins who were 'Out of Area' could be brought back for the week long camp which would effectively be used to cut the squad down from 50 to 25, so it was taken very seriously indeed. All the necessary bits were tied up to ensure everybody was present and the faith in them and their professionalism was looked to.

As things began to unfold I really began to feel I was at home in this environment. I had the credibility to be there. I also had one eye on what I could bring to the future of RAF RL, with the new approaches and skills I was picking up during this time.

A further day conditioning event was held in March and we knew how the lads were doing and who was taking things on professionally, so to be told that the RAF lads were streets ahead by the Kettlebell guys made me really proud.

Placing the ownership on players to achieve their own professional standards and abilities is something we in RAF RL have done for many years. So when June arrived and we knew we had to cut the squad down by half, which was going to be really tough, I was confident the majority of our players would get through. And the fact that only one RAF player had not made the final 25, having struggled with an injury, was pleasing. I was honest with him and he took it well. It was very hard, but you have to keep moving on.

Colchester may not be many people's venue of choice when it comes to spending three weeks of the summer, but that was the GB home and venue for the Armed Forces World Cup and we were set up there four days before our first hit up against New Zealand. The intensity of work rate and constant preparation was a first to me. It was similar to being on tour, but to see Wayne, Richie and a guy called Jason 'The Sheriff' Steele, the appointed team manager, working to full affect, doing all the jobs that I as RAF head coach would be focusing on as well as my actual role, was amazing. It freed me up to single-mindedly do the job I needed to do.

Inevitably I found myself looking at those other bits and worrying about them, which I found difficult. I was sort of conflicted. I did not want to step on anyone's toes. The support staff were incredible, but sometimes I found myself out of sorts and not knowing where to go or what to do - I thoroughly enjoyed it!

The event itself was excellent and I was amazed that all the teams actually turned up despite the costs and the current financial restraints and difficulties in the world. I'm certain that without the dedication of Deano and the support afforded by 16 Air Assault Brigade it would have been a non-starter.

With NZ, Australia, ourselves and Serbia the teams fighting it out for the event, a round robin tournament was to be held, and from the off the whole experience for me was of a step or two above what I was used to. Working alongside Wayne was great, and also the support staff and the players. Everybody gave everything and the atmosphere around the event was excellent.

Winning our first game against NZ, 32-8, was a great way to start. We then cruised past Serbia and had an almighty battle against the Aussies.

That match, for me, proved all our work was correct and worthwhile. Coming back from 20-4 down at half-time to lose by just one score gave us, I felt, a moral victory and showed our fitness was better than the other teams. But having lost to Australia, we faced the tougher of the two semi finals clashes against NZ and I think this was the only point where we made a mistake.

To all intents and purposes we - not out loud, but inside - all thought we were already in the final. The game was tough as expected, but we took our eye off the ball and once the final whistle had blown with the Kiwis winning 20-16, we knew the true cost of that mistake. We were focusing on what we would put right against the Aussies in the final, instead of the game in front of us.

Reflecting on it afterwards with Wayne, the players could not have done anymore, but a few odd referee decisions for forward passes I believe cost us dearly as well.

That is not sour grapes, far from it. We were clearly told before the tournament by the match commissionaires that we would be playing under 'international rules'.

Now, one of the differences between GB rules and International rules is that you are allowed to shoulder charge. There are others, but that rule proved costly to us as, during the semi-final, one of our lads put in a massive hit on a Kiwi player and the referee gave a penalty.

We got on the radio to argue that it was a legal hit, but we now found ourselves defending on our own 10-yard line. This is a World Cup semi-final and the referee didn't know what was going on. We lost our momentum and a string of mistakes, knock-ons, high tackles and so on cost us. With the match closing in we had a try disallowed due to a forward pass. We then scored, were winning 16-14 and thought we were home and hosed. But from a knock on from the kick-off they scored again, in the corner. With two minutes left, that was that.

The feeling afterwards - that one of total disbelief - has been echoed throughout out sport since its birth in 1895, and such emotions make it the wonderful game that it is.

## Through Adversity

You use it as education and I now know that being in that environment is where I want to be. Instead of Damian Clayton seeing the next step for himself as Head of the GB coaching set up and going to Australia in 2015 to complete the perfect picture and win the GB versus ANZACs 100th anniversary match, I can now only see myself doing that alongside Wayne, not as head, but as assistant. The hunger is there from both of us to make this new partnership work to the best of our abilities; to achieve the greatest triumph and to push each other as far as we can.

I'd be confident if I was selected head coach, but will be more than happy to be there with Wayne, train better and go one step further. As someone I've been friends with since this whole Service rugby league story began and played against in the first IS matches, to have now worked with him at such an important tournament has been excellent.

You live, learn and grow as a person. I have within the sport and the sport has allowed me to do that. I began to notice a lot of shifts in my personal landscape, something that I may not have done years ago.

Wayne and I are of similar stock, our passion and history in and of the game is the same. He is a Lancashire lad, I am Yorkshire. We have both been awarded an MBE for services to rugby league and we have also both been awarded the Combined Services Sports Official of the Year award. So maybe it would be fitting that our Service careers, in which we have held a torch for rugby league in one way or another, would see us travel to Australia in 2015 and win.

Watch this space ... Per Ardua!

*The End*

# All - Party Parliamentary Rugby League Group

HOUSE OF COMMONS
LONDON SW1A 0AA

DH/MH                    09 May 1996

Dear Colleague,

The next meeting of the All Party Parliamentary Rugby League Group will be held on _Wednesday 15th May at 6.00pm in Committee Room 12._

The speakers will be Martin Coyd, Army Rugby League and Damian Clayton, RAF Rugby League Association.

I hope you will be able to attend.

Yours sincerely,

David Hinchliffe MP
Joint Secretary.

CC MC DC
1

Investigate our other titles and
stay up to date with all our latest releases at
www.scratchingshedpublishing.co.uk